404 Deskside Activities for Energetic Kids

About the Author

A nationally recognized teacher, trainer, and choreographer for athletes and dancers, Barbara Davis spent much of her life making exercise an integral part of daily life for others. Armed with an MFA in Dance/Pilates and a Master of Science in Exercise Physiology, she coached and taught gymnastics for over twenty years and was the coauthor and national clinician for USA Kinder Accreditation for Teachers (KAT). She developed a movement program for ADHD children that is used by gymnastics schools across the United States and coauthored a book called *Teaching Fundamental Gymnastics Skills* in which she was responsible for developing verbal learning cues for specific learning styles. Barbara's contributions to gymnastics, exercise, and education were exceptional; she was able to present sports in a way that helped everyone learn, whether they were an elite athlete or a beginning student. Barbara Davis passed away in 2007 in Columbus, Ohio, where she lived with her husband Mark.

SmartFun Books from Hunter House

101 Music Games for Children by Jerry Storms
101 More Music Games for Children by Jerry Storms
101 Dance Games for Children by Paul Rooyackers
101 More Dance Games for Children by Paul Rooyackers
101 Drama Games for Children by Paul Rooyackers
101 More Drama Games for Children by Paul Rooyackers
101 Movement Games for Children by Huberta Wiertsema
101 Language Games for Children by Paul Rooyackers
101 Improv Games for Children by Bob Bedore
Yoga Games for Children by Danielle Bersma and Marjoke Visscher
The Yoga Adventure for Children by Helen Purperhart
101 Life Skills Games for Children by Bernie Badegruber
101 More Life Skills Games for Children by Bernie Badegruber
101 Family Vacation Games by Shando Varda
101 Cool Pool Games for Children by Kim Rodomista
404 Deskside Activites for Energetic Kids by Barbara Davis, MS, MFA
101 Relaxation Games for Children by Allison Bartl
101 Pep-Up Games for Children by Allison Bartl
101 Quick-Thinking Games + Riddles for Children by Allison Bartl
The Yoga Zoo Adventure by Helen Purperhart

Ordering

Trade bookstores in the U.S. and Canada please contact:

Publishers Group West
1700 Fourth St., Berkeley CA 94710
Phone: (800) 788-3123   Fax: (510) 528-3444

Hunter House books are available at bulk discounts for textbook course adoptions; to qualifying community, health-care, and government organizations; and for special promotions and fund-raising. For details please contact:

Special Sales Department
Hunter House Inc., PO Box 2914, Alameda CA 94501-0914
Phone: (510) 865-5282   Fax: (510) 865-4295
E-mail: ordering@hunterhouse.com

Individuals can order our books from most bookstores, by calling **(800) 266-5592**, or from our website at
www.hunterhouse.com

404
Deskside Activities for Energetic Kids

Barbara Peterson Davis, MS, MFA

A Hunter House SmartFun Book

Copyright © 2008 by Barbara Davis

All rights reserved. No part of this publication may be reproduced or transmitted in any form or by any means, electronic or mechanical, including photocopying and recording, or introduced into any information storage and retrieval system without the written permission of the copyright owner and the publisher of this book. Brief quotations may be used in reviews prepared for inclusion in a magazine, newspaper, or for broadcast. For further information please contact:

Hunter House Inc., Publishers
PO Box 2914
Alameda CA 94501-0914

Library of Congress Cataloging-in-Publication Data

Davis, Barbara, 1953 Feb. 16-
404 deskside activities for energetic kids / Barbara Peterson Davis. — 1st ed.
p. cm. (SmartFun activity books)
ISBN-13: 978-0-89793-467-1 (pbk.)
ISBN-10: 0-89793-467-9 (pbk.)
ISBN-13: 978-0-89793-468-8 (spiral bound)
ISBN-10: 0-89793-468-7 (spiral bound)
1. Education, Primary—Activity programs.   2. Active learning.   3. Activity programs in education.   4. Movement education.   I. Title.   II. Title: Four hundred and four deskside activities for energetic kids.
LB1027.25.D38 2006
372.86'8—dc22   2006021294

Project Credits

Cover Design: Jil Weil & Stefanie Gold
Cover Illustrator: Jeff Duckworth
Photographer: Coral Day-Davis
Photograph Editor: Alexis McQuilkin
Book Production: Hunter House/
   John McKercher
Copy Editor: Kelley Blewster
Proofreader: Herman Leung
Acquisitions Editor: Jeanne Brondino
Editor: Alexandra Mummery

Senior Marketing Associate: Reina Santana
Publicity Assistant: Alexi Ueltzen
Interns: Amy Hagelin and Julia Wang
Rights Coordinator: Candace Groskreutz
Customer Service Manager:
   Christina Sverdrup
Order Fulfillment: Washul Lakdhon
Administrator: Theresa Nelson
Computer Support: Peter Eichelberger
Publisher: Kiran S. Rana

Printed and Bound by Bang Printing, Brainerd, Minnesota

Manufactured in the United States of America

9 8 7 6 5 4 3 2 1   First Edition   08 09 10 11 12

Contents

Foreword xxii
Preface xxv

Introduction

Why Use Deskside Activities?. 1
The Teacher's Role. 3
Teaching Styles 4
Children's Learning Styles. 6
How to Use This Book 11
Key to the Icons Used in the Activities. 14

The Activities

Shape Recognition and Replication 18
Wake Up, Shake, Stretch, and Strengthen. 30
Creativity with the Body 43
Sports and Gymnastics. 96
Rhythm, Math, and Science 122

References 142
Activities with Special Requirements. 143

List of Games

		Preschool–mid-elementary	Kindergarten–mid-elementary	Early-elementary–mid-elementary
Page	Game			

Shape Recognition and Replication

Circles
20	Shoulder Circles	•		
20	Wrist Circles	•		
20	Elbow Circles	•		
20	Arm Circles	•		
21	Paint the Sky	•		
21	Finger Circles	•		
21	Foot Circles	•		
22	Knee Circles	•		
22	Body Circles	•		

Stars
22	Standing Star	•		
22	Desk Star	•		
23	Foreign Star	•		
23	Floor Star	•		
23	Sideward Star	•		
23	Star in the Sky	•		

Lines
24	Birthday Line	•		
24	Name Line	•		
24	Initials			•
24	Shoe Line	•		
25	Color Line	•		

vi ... 404 Deskside Activities for Energetic Kids

		Preschool–mid-elementary	Kindergarten–mid-elementary	Early-elementary–mid-elementary
Page	Game			

Curves
25	Paint a Curve in the Sky	•		
25	Paint a Rainbow	•		
25	Big Rainbow	•		
26	Group Rainbow	•		

Figure 8s
26	Tiny 8s		•	
26	Hand 8s		•	
26	Thumb 8s		•	
27	Big 8s		•	
27	Finger 8s		•	
27	Knee 8s		•	
27	Toe 8s		•	
27	Heel 8s		•	

Alphabet Shapes
28	Diagonal		•	
28	Triangle		•	
28	Circle	•		
28	Body Alphabet		•	
29	Foot Alphabet		•	
29	Standing Letters		•	
29	Partner Letters		•	
29	Giant Letters		•	
29	Hand-Painted Letters		•	

Wake Up, Shake, Stretch, and Strengthen

Shake Up
31	Hands	•		
31	Feet	•		
31	Legs	•		
31	Crazy Shakin'	•		

Page	Game	Preschool–mid-elementary	Kindergarten–mid-elementary	Early-elementary–mid-elementary

Wall Exercises
32	Wall Touch	•		
32	Wall Sit	•		
32	Wall Push-Up		•	
33	Diving Arms	•		

Wake Up, Stretch, and Relax
33	Yes/No	•		
33	Pigeon	•		
33	Giraffe Necks	•		
34	Diamonds and Ovals		•	
34	Wrist Stretches	•		
34	Turtle Heads (Wrist Movement)	•		
34	Mototcycle Hands	•		
34	Drummers	•		
35	Fruit Un-Roll-Ups	•		
35	Pizza Platters	•		
35	Spider Story	•		
36	Pencils and Erasers	•		
36	Flex and Point Balance	•		
36	Windshield-Wiper Feet	•		
36	Puzzle Feet		•	
36	Piano Toes			•
37	Foot Bridges		•	
37	Giant Spider	•		
37	Cat Stretch	•		
38	Rubber Band	•		
38	Neck Stretch		•	
38	Elephant Ears (Arms and Shoulders)	•		
38	Scratch Your Back	•		
39	Straight Arms	•		

viii ... 404 Deskside Activities for Energetic Kids

Page	Game	Preschool–mid-elementary	Kindergarten–mid-elementary	Early-elementary–mid-elementary
39	Calves and Backs of Legs	•		
39	Side Stretch	•		
39	Hamstring Stretch	•		
39	Achilles Stretch	•		
40	Shoulder Stretch	•		
40	Square Stretch	•		
40	Foot and Ankle Stretch		•	
41	Teepee		•	
41	Wake Up, Go to Sleep	•		
41	Book Lifting	•		
41	Row Relay	•		
42	Toss and Answer	•		
42	Desk Dominoes	•		

Creativity with the Body

Animal Activities

Page	Game	Preschool–mid-elementary	Kindergarten–mid-elementary	Early-elementary–mid-elementary
45	Elephant	•		
45	Penguin	•		
45	Rabbit	•		
45	Gorilla	•		
46	Crab Walk	•		
46	Crab Push-Ups	•		
46	Inchworm	•		
46	Birdstand	•		
46	Duck Walk	•		
47	Pigeon Walk	•		
47	Flamingo	•		
47	Sandpiper	•		
47	Bunny Jump	•		
48	Bear Walk	•		
48	Baby Bear Walk	•		

		Preschool–mid-elementary	Kindergarten–mid-elementary	Early-elementary–mid-elementary
Page	*Game*			
48	Camel Walk	•		
48	Roly-Poly Bug	•		
49	Caterpillar Roll	•		
49	Jellyfish	•		
49	Gator Walk	•		
49	Cat Leap	•		
49	Wolf Stand	•		
50	Cow Running	•		
50	Horse Gallop	•		
50	Giraffe *Chassé*	•		
50	Seal Support	•		
51	Hungry Seal	•		
51	Frog Jump	•		
51	Monkey Walk	•		
51	Monkey with a Tail in the Air	•		
52	Rhino Walk	•		
52	Horse Kick	•		
52	Mule Kick	•		
52	Spider Walk	•		

Walks

Simple Walks

53	Low Walk/High Walk	•		
53	Center Walk	•		
54	Toe-Ball-Heel Walk		•	
54	March	•		
54	Peanut Butter	•		
54	Weather Walk	•		
55	Head Walks		•	
55	Torso Walks		•	

x ... 404 Deskside Activities for Energetic Kids

Page	Game	Preschool–mid-elementary	Kindergarten–mid-elementary	Early-elementary–mid-elementary
55	Puppet Walks	•		
55	Arm and Shoulder Walks		•	

Character Walks

56	Toddler		•	
56	Wearing a Cast		•	
56	Old Walk		•	
56	Emotional Walk		•	
57	I'm Late!			•
57	Mad		•	
57	Look Out!	•		
57	Waiting		•	

Pantomime

58	I'm Melting	•		
58	Popcorn	•		
58	Tall Grass	•		
58	Wave	•		
59	Balloon	•		
59	Train	•		
59	Pretzel	•		
60	Leaning Tower of Pisa		•	
60	Top	•		
60	Ocean Plants	•		
60	Washing Machine	•		
60	Egg Beater	•		
61	Bouncing Ball	•		

Tasks

61	Rise and Shine	•		
61	Bed		•	
61	Morning Activities		•	

*404 Deskside Activities for Energetic Kids ... **xi***

Page	Game	Preschool–mid-elementary	Kindergarten–mid-elementary	Early-elementary–mid-elementary
62	Walk the Dog		•	
62	Doing Dishes		•	
62	Clothes		•	
62	Clean the House		•	
62	Picking Apples	•		
63	Cooking		•	
63	Midnight Drink		•	

Imagine

Page	Game			
63	Clouds		•	
63	Puddles	•		
64	Picking Flowers	•		
64	Caged		•	
64	Kickboxer		•	
64	Ant		•	
64	Reach for the Cookies	•		
65	Strong Man		•	
65	Hands Up!			•
65	Dinosaur	•		

Finger Animals

Page	Game			
65	Turkey		•	
66	Snail		•	
66	Fish	•		
66	Clam	•		
66	Anteater		•	
66	Bird	•		
67	Bat	•		
67	Chicken		•	
67	Two Deer Eating Leaves		•	

xii ... 404 Deskside Activities for Energetic Kids

Page	Game	Preschool–mid-elementary	Kindergarten–mid-elementary	Early-elementary–mid-elementary
	Movement Adventure			
	Fly to Africa			
68	Fly to Africa	•		
68	Land the Airplane	•		
68	Sunrise	•		
69	Tall Grass in the Wind	•		
	Wake Up			
69	Sleepy Ostriches	•		
70	Hungry Giraffes	•		
70	Flowers	•		
70	Seeds to Flowers	•		
70	Clouds	•		
71	Rain	•		
71	Tent	•		
71	Body Rap	•		
73	Clear Sky	•		
73	Butterfly	•		
73	Put on the Brakes	•		
73	Flower Sit-Ups	•		
74	Zebra	•		
74	Sandwich Sit-Ups	•		
75	Giant Sandwich	•		
76	Spider Sit-Ups	•		
76	Jungle River	•		
	Out to Sea			
77	A Sailor Went to Sea	•		
77	Jumping Sailor	•		
77	Jumping Criss-Cross Sailor			•
77	Classroom Wave	•		

*404 Deskside Activities for Energetic Kids ... **xiii***

Page	Game	Preschool–mid-elementary	Kindergarten–mid-elementary	Early-elementary–mid-elementary
78	Mer-People Workout	•		
78	Sea Horses	•		
78	Sea Anemones	•		
78	Sharks	•		
79	Flying Fish	•		

To the Moon

Page	Game			
79	Rocket to the Moon	•		
79	Feeling Floaty	•		
79	Balance on the Moon	•		
80	Big Kicks on the Moon	•		
80	Tiptoe Around the Crater	•		
80	Jumps on the Moon	•		
80	Back to Earth	•		

Back on Earth

Page	Game			
81	Looking for an Elephant	•		
84	Relaxation Exercise	•		

Shapes and Statues

Simple Shapes and Statues

Page	Game			
85	Famous Statues		•	
85	Everyday Shapes		•	
85	Make Your Favorite Shapes		•	
85	Tall/Low Shapes		•	
86	Wide Shape		•	
86	Round Shape		•	
86	Square Shape		•	
86	Angled Shape		•	
87	Flat Shape		•	
87	Twisted Shape		•	

Base of Support

Page	Game			
87	One Base		•	

Page	Game	Preschool–mid-elementary	Kindergarten–mid-elementary	Early-elementary–mid-elementary
87	Two Bases		•	
87	One Hand, Two Feet		•	
87	Two Hands, One Leg		•	
88	Head, Hand, Foot		•	
88	Elbows		•	
88	Side		•	
88	Twenty Bases	•		

Open and Closed Spaces

Page	Game	Preschool	Kindergarten	Early-elementary
88	Open Spaces		•	
88	Closed Spaces		•	
89	Symmetry and Asymmetry	•		

Kaleidoscope (Moving with Shapes)

Page	Game	Preschool	Kindergarten	Early-elementary
89	Shape Pattern		•	
89	Up-and-Down Shape	•		
89	Forward/Backward Shape		•	
90	Circular Floor Pattern	•		
90	Machine Shape		•	
90	Sideward Shape		•	
90	Mirror Shape		•	
91	Inverted Shape		•	
91	Partner Shape		•	
91	Shifting Shape		•	
91	Jungle Gym	•		

Reactions

Page	Game	Preschool	Kindergarten	Early-elementary
92	Dart-Slither		•	
92	Balance-Explode		•	
92	Sit-Jump	•		
92	Float-Drip		•	
93	Whirl-Vibrate		•	
93	Press-Pop	•		

404 Deskside Activities for Energetic Kids ... xv

		Preschool–mid-elementary	Kindergarten–mid-elementary	Early-elementary–mid-elementary
Page	Game			
93	Stamp-Swing		•	
93	Stop and Go	•		
93	Combination: Stop and Go and Touch the Floor	•		

Isolation of Body Parts

94	Body Parts	•		
94	Body Part to Body Part	•		
94	Slow Motion	•		

General Reactions

94	Follow the Leader (Shadow)	•		
95	Mirror Image		•	
95	Side by Side		•	

Sports and Gymnastics

Baseball

97	Throwing	•		
98	Pitch	•		
98	Outfield		•	
98	Holding the Bat	•		
98	Swing the Bat		•	
99	Swing, Twist			•
99	Follow Through			•

Underarm Swing

99	Bowling	•		
99	Underarm Swing	•		
100	Underarm Swing, Lunge		•	
100	Step, Underarm Swing, Lunge			•
100	Softball Pitch	•		

Basketball

101	Hold, Bend, Shoot		•	
101	Jump and Shoot	•		

Page	Game	Preschool–mid-elementary	Kindergarten–mid-elementary	Early-elementary–mid-elementary
101	Jump Shot	•		
102	Dribble	•		
102	Bounce, Step, Bend, and Shoot		•	

Tennis, Anyone?

Page	Game			
102	Ready Position	•		
102	Handshake Grip		•	
103	Forearm Swing		•	
103	Backhand Swing		•	
103	Lob		•	
103	Serve		•	

Golf

Page	Game			
104	The Swing		•	
104	Weight Shift		•	
104	Full Swing		•	

Football

Page	Game			
105	Pass	•		
105	Punt	•		
105	Catching the Ball	•		
106	Jump and Catch		•	
106	Move to It			•
106	Jump, Catch, Look, and Pass			•
106	Pass Behind			•
106	Football Drills	•		

Bicycling

Page	Game			
107	Upside-Down Bicycles	•		

Swimming

Page	Game			
107	Crawl	•		
108	Back Stroke	•		
108	Side Stroke			•

404 Deskside Activities for Energetic Kids ... xvii

		Preschool–mid-elementary	Kindergarten–mid-elementary	Early-elementary–mid-elementary
Page	Game			
108	Breaststroke	•		
108	Butterfly Stroke			•

Sitting Positions

Page	Game			
109	Criss-Cross, Applesauce	•		
109	Tuck	•		
110	Open Pike, Closed Pike	•		
111	Straddle	•		
112	Three Bears' Rocking Chairs	•		
112	Stag (Side, Front, and Back)	•		
113	*Passé*	•		
113	V-Sit	•		

Standing Positions

Page	Game			
114	Straight Body	•		
114	Squat	•		
115	Straddle Stand	•		
115	Stride	•		
115	Lunge (Front, Side, Back)		•	
116	Standing Tuck to Standing Pike	•		
116	Thread the Needle			•
116	Hollow Body (Banana)/Arch		•	
117	Salute	•		
117	Pike Combination	•		

Supports

Page	Game			
118	Front Support	•		
118	Back Support		•	
118	Side Support	•		
119	Side Support in *Passé*			•
119	Side Support in Straddle (Side Star)			•
119	Compass Walk	•		
119	Support Combination			•

xviii ... 404 Deskside Activities for Energetic Kids

Page	Game	Preschool–mid-elementary	Kindergarten–mid-elementary	Early-elementary–mid-elementary
Holds				
120	Pretzel Hold	•		
120	Tuck Hold	•		
120	Straddle Hold	•		
121	Half L (Wolf Hold)		•	
121	L Hold	•		
121	V Hold	•		

Rhythm, Math, and Science

Page	Game	Preschool–mid-elementary	Kindergarten–mid-elementary	Early-elementary–mid-elementary
Arm Positions				
123	Crown	•		
123	Beach Ball	•		
124	Low Round	•		
124	Oblique	•		
124	Opposition			•
124	Side Middle (T Shape)	•		
125	Jazz First	•		
125	English Hands			•
Balances				
125	Ruler/Eraser Balances	•		
125	Walking Erasers			•
126	Tuck Stand	•		
126	*Relevé*	•		
126	Elevator	•		
127	Knee Stand	•		
127	Kneel	•		
127	Knee Scale	•		
127	Free Knee Scale		•	
128	Standing *Passé*	•		
128	Thigh Balance	•		
128	*Coupé*		•	

404 Deskside Activities for Energetic Kids ... xix

Page	Game	Preschool–mid-elementary	Kindergarten–mid-elementary	Early-elementary–mid-elementary
128	Hokey Pokey Challenge	•		

Dance Positions and Scales

Page	Game	Preschool–mid-elementary	Kindergarten–mid-elementary	Early-elementary–mid-elementary
129	Pizza Slice (First Position)		•	
130	First and Second Poem	•		
130	Back Scale	•		
131	Side Scale	•		
131	Front Scale	•		
131	Y-Scale		•	
131	Front/Back Attitude	•		
131	T-Scale	•		
132	Lever (Teeter-Totter)		•	

Turns

Page	Game	Preschool–mid-elementary	Kindergarten–mid-elementary	Early-elementary–mid-elementary
132	Sit and Spin	•		
132	Tuck-Stand Turn	•		
132	Pivot Turn	•		
133	Elevator Up and Down	•		
133	*Soutenu*		•	

Jumps

Page	Game	Preschool–mid-elementary	Kindergarten–mid-elementary	Early-elementary–mid-elementary
133	Safe Landing Position (SLP)	•		
134	Stretch Jump	•		
134	Jumping Fractions (Half-Turn Jumps)		•	
134	More Jumping Fractions (Quarter-Turn Jumps)	•		
135	Full-Turn Jumps	•		
135	Tuck Jump	•		
135	Straddle Jump	•		
135	Hitch Kick	•		
136	Jump Combination	•		
136	Pike Jump		•	
136	*Assemblé*		•	
136	*Sissoné*			•

Page	Game	Preschool–mid-elementary	Kindergarten–mid-elementary	Early-elementary–mid-elementary
136	Split Jump	•		
137	Front, Back, and Double Stag Jumps		•	
137	Herds of Deer	•		

Rhythm and Clapping Games

Page	Game			
137	Steady Beat	•		
137	Peter Works	•		
138	Echo		•	
138	My Name Symphony		•	
138	Full Name Symphony		•	
138	Echo My Name		•	
139	1 and 3, 2 and 4			•
139	Off Beat			•
139	Choose the Beats			•

Math and Science

Page	Game			
139	Human Links: Addition	•		
139	Human Links: Subtraction	•		
140	Human Division		•	
140	Human Sets	•		
140	Human Links: Multiplication			•
140	Human Links: Division			•
140	Planets Rotating		•	
141	Solar System		•	

404 Deskside Activities for Energetic Kids ... xxi

Foreword

I have known Barbara Davis as a friend, teacher, colleague, teammate, consultant, and visionary. Her dedication to the fitness and wellness of children spans decades and is evidenced by her outstanding and award-winning work in the field and in publications and videos. Her experience is as vast as it is diverse, encompassing personal performance, training world-class athletes, and teaching young children in schools and gyms around the country.

I began my teaching career in the late 1960s in my native Scotland, where I taught kindergarten for several years before moving to the United States and completing my undergraduate and graduate degrees. At that time, British education was going through an exciting change, with sweeping reforms and a strong movement toward child-centered teaching. I met Barbara in the mid 1990s, when we were both teaching at the University of Central Florida. I was the director of the early-childhood teacher-education program, and Barbara taught in the fitness lab. We were drawn to each other immediately by our common concerns about the direction in which many early-childhood programs in public schools were heading. We discussed the trend in primary classrooms toward highly structured instruction, too often characterized by ditto sheets, workbooks, and minimal interaction among children. Tests and measurements and the "back to basics" movement seemed to us to be overshadowing the needs of children. We both believed that these trends would serve to switch children off and create failure. Another common concern was the number of children who were being diagnosed as having ADHD, and who were subsequently medicated at an early age. We felt that many of these children, particularly boys, were being victimized by a system of schooling that placed inappropriate expectations on them. An inappropriate environment is one in which too much is expected of children too soon.

Barbara supported me in my desire to open an innovative charter school that would be child-centered and developmentally appropriate, and where a creative, dynamic curriculum would be developed according to the needs of the children, rather than being driven by textbooks and tests. In this school, children would be free to move about, to interact with their environment, teachers, and peers, to make choices, and to be active participants in their education. In 2000, I opened the Campus Charter School in Port St. John, Florida. Barbara developed and taught the music and movement program at the school until she moved with her family to Ohio in 2002. During those two years, I was privileged to observe firsthand her work with young children. Her joy in her work was apparent, as was her genuine love of children. Her creativity, sensitivity, and expertise enhanced the life of every child she taught. I am proud to say that some of the activities in this book were developed and refined as she worked with the children at Campus Charter School. The school is now in its eighth year of successful operation, and it still operates according to the ideals Barbara and I believe in so fervently.

In general, the situation for children in public schools in the United States does not seem to have improved over the past decade. In too many classrooms, a number of educationally inappropriate practices have become common, such as long periods of sitting and listening, skill and drill practice, and emphasis on preparation for standardized testing. Developmentally appropriate practices and policies have given way to lessons geared toward preparation for state tests. In many states around the country, formal standardized testing does not begin until third grade, but it is not uncommon to see children in kindergarten, first grade, and second grade feeling the pressure of the state tests as the test-driven curriculum is pushed down to the earliest school years. Daily schedules have become more and more restrictive as pressure is put on teachers to prepare children for tests. Teachers are confronted with the dilemma of choosing between what they believe is appropriate for their students and what their administrators feel is necessary for higher achievement scores on state tests. Teachers feel judged by results. As a consequence, children are required to sit at desks doing paper-and-pencil tasks for longer periods of time than ever before. Children are movers, and as such will always find it very difficult to stay still in classrooms where very little movement is encouraged or tolerated. Often, teachers ask children to stand up and stretch, do jumping jacks or other rapid movements to "shake out their wiggles." Such activity, with lack of meaningful purpose, can overexcite children and have quite the opposite effect of the one teachers hope for! Children may find it difficult to settle back down to work after such vigorous movement. Unfortunately, teachers are often at a loss as to what to do to offer appropriate movement activities to their students. They are also very aware that every minute of the school day is viewed as instructional time, and that any movement activity must be viewed by supervisors and administrators as having educational value.

404 Deskside Activities for Energetic Kids is the teacher's manual for combining creative movement and educational objectives in the classroom. Barbara's book provides step-by-step instructions for teachers on how to facilitate opportunities for children to use their bodies in joyous and creative ways so they can develop confidence, self-esteem, a positive body image, and an active lifestyle.

The book's activities are thematically organized and are ordered according to level of difficulty. The activities are coded with symbols or icons that give the teacher important information at a glance, such as the appropriate age group, the size of the group needed, if the task is advanced, if props are required, if a large space is needed, if the game requires students to possess skills learned in earlier activities, or if physical contact is or might be involved. Each activity is based on a firm understanding of children's physiology, so that teachers can be confident that no child will be asked to move in a way that is not safe and appropriate. Even more important, the book is written in easy-to-understand language that guides even the most inexperienced teacher in rewarding and fun movement activities.

— Elaine Clifford, Ph.D.

Preface

Many children in today's Western society no longer have movement opportunities built into their daily activities. As a child I walked to school, climbed trees, rode my bike, played running games with my dog in our yard, and climbed into our hayloft in search of kittens. Modern life has removed much movement from children's days. Often it is not safe or feasible to walk to school or to bicycle to a friend's house for an afternoon of play. Most children can be divided into two camps: the overly sedentary ones who spend many hours in front of computers or televisions, and the ones who require lots of movement (high-mobility-need children). Both groups need to move. Many children begin the school day with too much pent-up energy and go through classes unable to release it. Most American children do not have a daily physical education class. We confine children to their desks for eight hours a day and yet are quick to label children with hyperactivity or attention deficit hyperactivity disorder (ADHD). It has been apparent to me as an elementary-school teacher and an instructor of dance and gymnastics that children in America's classrooms desperately need more activity and movement breaks.

This book is for preschool to third grade teachers who have classrooms full of energetic children—the ones who squirm in their seats and cannot pay continuous attention. It is also for teachers who have ADD or ADHD children in their classrooms. The book consists primarily of small movement breaks that are success oriented and educational yet fun and engaging—breaks that can help to bring children back to the task at hand or can help to keep them on task for longer periods of time. Most importantly, these activities can help to make movement a fun and significant part of children's daily lives and can help to optimize children's learning in the classroom through movement. The word "deskside" in the book's title is partly metaphorical; although most of the activities can be performed next to children's desks or tables, some call for traveling up and down the aisles or pushing desks back to create additional space.

Movement is essential to children's cognitive as well as physical development. A kinesthetic learning style is one of the eight learning styles (or "multiple intelligences") first proposed and described by educational psychologist Howard Gardner. These learning styles, outlined in the Introduction, are a widely accepted and applied theory about the ways in which children perceive and learn about the world. Most children are highly kinesthetic in their early years, always wanting to touch something to learn more about it and always wanting to move through or on things to explore them. Without physical engagement, some children, including ADHD children, may find it difficult to learn basic skills such as recognizing the alphabet.

The book's activities are thematically organized, and they are ordered according to level of difficulty. The first chapter, "Shape Recognition and Replication," utilizes simple movements preschoolers can easily perform. The later chapters will help to develop coordination and build on previous activities. Because many activities can be done on their own, you can do the activities in the order in which they are presented or randomly choose ones appropriate for your group. Where experience or knowledge of previous activities is needed, I have indicated so.

Use of this activity book is not limited to the regular classroom. I encourage all adults who work with children to utilize it in after-school programs, day-care facilities, church groups, camps, recreation centers, and gymnastic centers—virtually anywhere children need movement breaks and activities. I hope you will use this material often and that it will refresh you and your children.

Introduction

Why Use *Deskside Activities?*

Movement provides children with a necessary energetic outlet during a fairly sedentary school day. As mentioned in the Preface, modern daily life provides children with many fewer opportunities for movement than was the case even a generation ago. Children need to use their bodies in joyous and creative ways so that they can develop confidence, self-esteem, a positive body image, and an active lifestyle.

The activities in this book can also enhance the following areas of child development:

Physical Development

Parents rely largely on the school systems to educate their children intellectually and physically. Yet most children in public schools have physical education classes only once or twice a week, and much of the burden of providing activity is left to the classroom teacher or to the after-school and day-care teachers. These individuals can lead children through positive movement experiences that will help them develop a love of activity and movement that may carry over into a healthy attitude toward exercise as they grow into teenagers and adults.

Social Development

Learning to move within a group helps children to become more aware of one another. As they develop spatial awareness they will adjust their movement patterns to stay clear of one another and to avoid collisions.

Empathy is another worthy byproduct of cooperative endeavors. Learning about people's strengths and weaknesses or movement limitations can be a very valuable lesson. And in physically imagining how to move like animals, children can develop appreciation, respect, and compassion for them.

Cognitive Development

All of the activities in *404 Deskside Activities for Energetic Kids* have educational value, and many offer more than simply movement education. Teachers can utilize the activities to create unique learning experiences for their students. For instance, natural science can be combined with movement exploration in activities that involve impressions of animal walks. And geometrical shapes are the focus of many activities in the book.

When learning to write, children will be much less likely to reverse letters and numbers if they have a solid understanding of laterality (sidedness within the body, or right and left) and directionality (spatial awareness outside the body, or forward, backward, and sideward movement). For example, if children have cognitively and physically experienced front, back, and side lunges, they will be much less likely to reverse and confuse the letters b, d, p, and q. By the same token, if they have gone upside down or turned and rotated their body shapes, they will understand and be comfortable with such concepts as the inverting of fractions. That is precisely why the gymnastics section of the book is so large. Sometimes the most abstract of concepts such as retrograde and inversion can be taught very easily and concretely through movement.

Multiplication can be understood quite simply when children see other students in groups of twos, threes, and fours (human sets). And the concepts of rotation and revolution of the planets can be exemplified in a movement session with a child representing the sun by standing in the middle and turning around and around while other children, acting as the planets, revolve around her or him. For more advanced understanding, the children can also rotate as they revolve around the "sun," in accordance with the particular timing of their respective planet.

Creativity

As difficult as it is to imagine a world without creativity, it has been known for quite some time that Americans begin to lose creativity—the ability to improvise and play dramatically without being self-conscious—at around age five (Dudek 1974). It is not surprising that this is the exact age at which children all begin to learn the same curriculum, to take standardized tests, and to sit at desks for most of their day. The willingness to be creative suffers drastic reduction again at approximately age nine (fourth grade), the age at which the results of the standardized tests become so important. Most of America's schools are under great pressure to have their children do well in the fourth grade standardized test series. Again, creativity drops markedly at age twelve, or in the seventh grade, when the final exit from childhood to middle school or junior high takes place. If children continue to engage in physical dramatic play throughout their early elementary years they will continue to feel more comfortable and confident about themselves as they progress through adolescence and puberty. Somehow the increasing demand for academic accountability and competition wrings most of the creativity out of children as they grow up. Yet success, not just in the arts but also in science and business, often depends on staying abreast of the latest innovations and approaches. Keeping dramatic and improvisational creativity alive in the classroom not only will aid children in actively thinking and problem solving on their own, but also will help them carry that mindset into their futures. It should be noted that the ages suggested are only that—suggestions. Children progress at different ages.

Movement exploration is inherently creative, as is obvious if you've ever watched a stageful of dancers doing identical moves. Each individual brings his or her special qualities to the steps—the unique way of moving through space that causes one dancer's style to be described as "explosive" and another's as "fluid." Many of the activities in this book prescribe exactly how to do certain things—how to transform the body to look and move like a gorilla, say, or how to execute an overarm throw. Others call for improvisation. Both types of activities help children develop creativity by allowing them to sense how their body moves and how they can change the quality of that movement—from fast to slow, vigorous to flowing, etc.

The Teacher's Role

Maintaining a positive classroom environment is one of the most important aspects of using this book. Children who experience success in a friendly, fun, and encouraging atmosphere are less likely to become bored or to give up on assignments. "Compliment sandwiches" are an excellent way to keep children motivated:

1. Compliment the child or children.
2. Suggest a correction or new approach.
3. Encourage them to continue.

In a classroom of movement there must be rules for class management. Stating the rules proactively can be a challenge. Some important rules include:

1. Always follow the instructions.
2. Keep clear of others so that you avoid colliding.
3. Work quietly so that directions can be heard and you will know what to do next.

Children love to impress their cherished teachers, so using directive language such as "Can you show me…" or "Let me see you do…" will be tremendously helpful.

Making the transition out of a movement session that children really enjoy can be difficult, of course, especially for those who most need movement—for example, ADHD children. This has to be done with the promise of more movement sessions to come. The "if, then" approach can be of tremendous help here. For instance, "If we complete all of our math today, then we will have another movement session this afternoon."

Always remember that the most sedentary students need this kind of activity but also will be the most hesitant to participate. They will need constant encouragement. The following list of self-esteem exercises should be done often and may well be the most important exercises in the entire book! Choose one to do at the close of each movement session:

1. **Hug**
   Stand up and give yourself a great big hug.
2. **Pat on the Back**
   Stand up, give yourself a pat on the back, and say, "Good job, Me."
3. **WOW**
   Write "WOW" with your fingers:
   1. Tips of thumbs together with pointer fingers extended
   2. Pointers and thumbs together
   3. Tips of thumbs together with pointer fingers extended
4. **Finger Applause**
   Give yourself a pinkie applause (both pinkies together), then a pointer applause, then a thumbkin applause, etc.
5. **Silent Cheer**
   Do a silent cheer by lifting your arms straight above your head, opening your mouths, and pantomiming an uproarious cheer.
6. **Round of Applause**
   Give yourself a round of applause by clapping your hands together in a circular pattern in front of you.
7. **Vertical Clapping**
   Applaud yourself first with your right hand on top and then with your left hand on top.
8. **Crown Yourself**
   Make yourself king or queen for the moment by creating a crown with your arms (elbows up and bent with fingers touching your head). Make an even bigger crown for yourself by extending your arms straight overhead.
9. **Foot Applause**
   Give yourself some foot applause by tapping your toes on the floor.
10. **Take a Bow**
    Stand up, place one hand on your waist, and graciously take a bow.

Teaching Styles

Next it is necessary to consider how to teach movement to a group of children, especially if the teacher doesn't have a background in movement education. Below are three types of teaching styles often utilized in movement education. You may consider incorporating these methods to enhance your sessions.

Direct/Command Approach

In this teaching approach the teacher makes all the decisions. While this is a very authoritative approach, it may well be the most desirable one to use at first, particularly if students and teacher are new to classroom movement sessions. This style creates a highly controlled and structured environment. In this sense it affords a large degree of class management.

This type of leadership provides unison in movement while also teaching valuable lessons. According to Mosston and Ashworth (1990), "Emulating, repeating, copying and responding to directions seem to be necessary ingredients of the early years." Unison clapping, finger plays, and mirroring activities, as well as all the movements in the first four chapters, can be taught using this method.

Another advantage of this style is that the teacher sees the results immediately. She or he can see whether or not the children understand and can follow the directions, and then can adjust accordingly.

Guided Exploration

Although this approach involves a more passive teaching style, it should be one of the most widely used techniques in movement sessions. Within this setting the teacher will give a suggestion or directive (e.g., "Show me a rounded or curved shape") and the children will explore making curved shapes until they have found their favorite one. The teacher can then suggest additional challenges to vary and extend the activity (e.g., "Can you turn your shape around?").

There are tremendous self-esteem benefits in teaching through this approach because every response is valid. The teachers are able to help in refining movements little by little through additional suggestions, varying the assignments just enough to keep children interested and challenged but also able to complete them. Teachers adopting this style must use their ability and foresight to choose problems and suggest extensions that are developmentally appropriate, both physically and intellectually, and that are relevant to the subject matter as well as to the children's lives (Cleland 1990). Teachers and coaches must provide the positive feedback and encouragement that young children need in order to keep going and to realize that there are many possibilities. This type of leadership requires time, patience, creativity, and practice, as well as careful verbal articulation. It works best when the teacher is comfortable with it, and it is absolutely magical when the teacher draws the children into the exploration to the extent that they are not focused on anything else.

Guided Discovery
This method, like guided exploration, is child-centered rather than teacher- or task-centered. The teacher may have a specific task or concept in mind and will provide the needed guidance and leadership while allowing the students to make decisions on their own. Within this approach the teacher will have enough control over the class to ensure learning and safety, but will pose challenges geared toward discovery or accomplishment of the activity. This process allows creativity and experimentation and yet guides the children as they converge on solutions.

Guided discovery is more time consuming than the direct approach, but many educators believe that the benefits are worth it. Within this approach the children not only learn the skills but they also learn all the interconnected parts of the skills. The most valuable benefit is that children learn how to learn while using this process. Through guided discovery children will learn how movements progress, fit together, and build upon one another within given movement sequences or tasks.

It is important for the teacher to avoid providing the answer. The children cannot "discover" the answer if it is given to them in the beginning or even along the way. Graham (1992) also maintains that because "wonder and curiosity are valuable mental processes," there is no harm in concluding a lesson in which the children have yet to discover the solution. For instance, the teacher could ask the children how they might make a fish or a turkey with their fingers. As the children discover ways to make the finger animals the teacher can suggest details of the animal's body such as the tail or the fin. If no one can figure out how to make an anteater with their fingers perhaps the teacher can tell the children to think about it overnight and then come back to the lesson the next day. Undoubtedly there will be responses to the assignment after twenty-four hours of creative juices flowing. The pantomiming and improvisational sections are perfect for guided discovery. The teacher can gently talk the students through movements of plants on the ocean floor or the process of climbing up to reach the cookies on the highest shelf.

Children's Learning Styles

The next issue to address is how to teach movement to individual children. In his book *Frames of Mind* (1983), Howard Gardner offers insight into teaching individual children as he identifies seven—since expanded to eight—different learning styles, also commonly known as "multiple intelligences." These learning styles are linguistic, musical, visual-spatial, kinesthetic, logical-mathematical, interpersonal, intrapersonal, and naturalistic.

In watching children behave, the observant teacher can see the types of cues to which different children respond and how strongly or weakly they respond to them. The teacher can then enhance the children's learning process by engaging their strengths as well as developing their weaknesses. In teaching children technical skills such as gymnastics moves, it may be important for teachers to describe the skill to each learning style. For example, in the pike position, the teacher can tell the kinesthetic student to feel his legs together and his knees squeezing tight to straighten his legs, but she might tell the visual student to see how straight her legs are. In an improvisation setting the teacher might only give verbal cues to help develop the listening skills of the less auditory children.

The primary learning categories of very young children (ages birth to five) are visual-spatial, auditory (which encompasses linguistic and musical), kinesthetic, and naturalistic. Preschool children can by and large be divided into two categories of learning styles. In general, preschool girls tend to be auditory learners, and preschool boys tend to be more visual-spatial in their perception and learning filtration. Auditory learners need verbal cues when learning new skills. These children need the teacher to literally talk them through a skill. The visual-spatial learners usually need demonstration of skills. Most Americans have been taught and tend to teach linguistically, expecting students to listen to verbal instructions. If a particular movement project requires extensive verbal instruction it would behoove preschool and kindergarten teachers to put the more auditory girls in the front row so that the visual-spatial boys have examples to follow. As children mature beyond age five and as they go through the educational process, they learn to use more than their dominant learning style.

Most young children are highly kinesthetic and, if put in the proper position or taken through a movement, will be able to feel the shape, timing, force, and flow of the movement or skill. For example, children will remember a tuck position because they can feel their thighs touching their chests.

The other, almost universal quality of young children is their love of nature. Their fascination with animals, bugs, weather, the sun, moon, and stars gives teachers an endless supply of engaging examples and metaphors. When teaching difficult movement skills to young children, always use the four primary categories of learning (visual-spatial, auditory, kinesthetic, and naturalistic). However, teachers should not only teach through students' learning strengths but also help to develop the other learning modes. For instance, a teacher may teach a *relevé* or tiptoe walk by telling the children to feel only the front of their feet touching the floor (kinesthetic), or by telling them to walk as quietly as they can (auditory), or by telling them to look down and see only their toes touching the floor (visual), or by telling them to walk as tall as they can (spatial), or by telling them to make the longest, tallest, straightest line that they can while they walk (mathematical/geometrical).

Below is a detailed discussion of the eight learning styles. The purpose of including this information is to help teachers be better teachers—to help them be able to describe movements in ways that are understandable to each type of perception, rather than sounding like the stereotypic gym teacher who gives the same verbal cues over and over while expecting better results.

Kinesthetic and Tactile

Most young children learn by touching, feeling, moving, and experiencing. There are many ways to teach kinesthetically and tactilely and to develop those sensibilities even in children who do not have them. ("Kinesthetic" refers to gross motor abilities and "tactile" to fine motor abilities.) Footprints and handprints made out of different textures will engage even the nonkinesthetic child. The already kinesthetic learners need to touch, feel, and move their way through a skill. They need to feel a skill on their own, much the same way intrapersonal learners need to make certain discoveries on their own. Often kinesthetic children do not like to be spotted (physically guided) through a skill because they will pay as much attention to the teacher's touch as they will to the skill they are trying to learn.

Kinesthetic children use full body movement and keep their heads and entire body weight very centered. Sometimes they stand with their hands folded across their chests and with legs slightly bent. They speak slowly, paced and with pauses.

Because the content of the book is movement, teaching through the kinesthetic style is appropriate, but remember that some of the children who need movement and exercise the most are the nonphysical types. The use of kinesthetic language (e.g., "feel your arms by your ears"; "squeeze the muscles above your knees tight"; "can you feel your big toes together, heels together, knees together?") will speak to the kinesthetic learners and also begin to develop the kinesthetic sense of the more sedentary children. Ask the children if their shoulders are up or down, forward or back. Ask them if their backs are straight. These phrases may have to be repeated several times to bring the nonkinesthetic types into a more sentient state.

Even though one might think that the ADHD child would be kinesthetic, close examination tells us that much of all that extraneous movement is unconscious (the constant tapping of feet, fidgeting, twirling the hair). The child has no awareness of these sometimes "annoying" tendencies. Therefore, it becomes extremely important to bring the ADHD child into a higher level of movement awareness. The typical ADHD child has problems grounding his paper with his nonwriting hand, and therefore the ambidexterity of exercises (doing each exercise on both the right and the left sides) is valuable. Quite commonly the ADHD child avoids crossing the midline of the body, so teachers can work on this weakness in Criss-Cross, Applesauce (#307), Pretzel (#145), and other exercises.

Linguistic

Linguistic learners, who learn primarily on a verbal basis, are often firstborn children who are surrounded by adult conversation and language. They will enjoy learning anatomical terms such as "biceps" and movement terms such as "extend," "flex," and "invert." These children sometimes actually respond physically to words; they will cherish, listen to, and remember the teacher's words. Our school systems tend to test linguistically, and since little girls are usually more linguistic, they test ready for school earlier than most boys of the same age do. When going through the units on body positions, assume a position and ask the boys to name the position. This will help the boys become more linguistically acute. Watch all the girls' hands go up in the air as the boys struggle to remember the names of each pose.

Visual-Spatial

Telling a young visual-spatial learner what to do will have little or no effect at all unless the skill is also demonstrated or some visual examples are given. Drawing mental pictures and giving spatial landmarks to these children is also very important. They will be able to draw a curve in the sky if they are told to draw rainbows with arms. They will be able to do a tuck jump if they are told to bring their knees up to their chests. "Lift your arms up to the sky" will work better than trying to tell them to straighten their arms. Color-coding also works extremely well; for example, "Put your feet on the grass and your hands on the blue mat."

The visual-spatial child looks observant; she or he can be seen focusing on something at all times. Visual kids speak at a rapid pace and in quick bursts of words. Sometimes they are so visual-spatial that they will go to the exact place where the teacher demonstrated the skill to reenact it because they can't separate the skill from the space in which it was done. Always give the visual-spatial child clear points of reference when describing which way to turn (e.g., "face the window"), and tell them where to look when executing a skill.

Musical

A musical learner can be identified very easily by turning on low-volume music in the background or by reciting a phrase rhythmically. The children whose heads turn and whose attention is taken by the sound are usually musical learners. The use of audio-tonal rhythm is very effective with these children. Making up little poems about a movement they are doing will engage these children.

Very young musical learners (even two-year-olds) will enjoy rhyming activities such as Knee Scale (#353).

The musical learners can also be identified by their postural stance. These children tend to lean forward as if they are trying to hear something. They are also the children who tend to readily sing in the classroom, sometimes unconsciously. The clapping of hands, snapping of fingers, and tapping out of rhythms are quite effective teaching tools for musical learners. They will appreciate being told what kinds of sounds and rhythms their hands and feet make during any given skill (e.g., you can show them how turning a cartwheel requires the steady rhythm of "hand, hand, foot, foot," and that a gallop goes "step, step, pause" or "knee, knee, pause" by having the children perform "clap, clap, pause; clap, clap, pause").

Interpersonal

This type of student works best by learning with others and by helping others learn at the same time that they themselves are learning. These children are peer motivated and have strong social needs. Permit or arrange for this type of child to work in pairs and to provide frequent interaction with his or her fellow students, such as mirroring, making partnered shapes, and playing cooperative games like relays. Teachers who have worked with interpersonal learners know that if they do not provide such scenarios, the students will create them, usually in a disruptive fashion. It is easy to be annoyed by interpersonal learners until one realizes that these students are not trying to be disruptive; they view being in the world as a series of interactions and learn more as well as have more fun learning that way. The interpersonal learners quite possibly may be future teachers. To facilitate learning for this type of student, it helps to remember that every activity can be mirrored ("mirror your pike with the pike of the person next to you").

Intrapersonal

The word "intrapersonal" literally translates as "from within." The intrapersonal learning style describes children who learn internally. This type of child tends to be self-motivated and learns best on his or her own. He or she is self-paced and self-checking.

These children work well when given projects (e.g., "practice this until your legs are straight"; "do five headstands against the wall and then come back for another assignment"; "practice inchworms until you have counted to fifty"; "do full-turn jumps until you can see yourself land in the mirror"). They also need to be allowed to explore skills on their own, even at the back of the room so that they can learn in their own medium. They will give themselves feedback and sometimes let others in on their findings. These children are the inductive reasoners of the future and need their own time in which to discover and explore.

Logical-Mathematical (and Digital)
These children are analytical and will need to be led through skills step by step. Although these students used to be in the minority of preschool through early-elementary children, the percentage keeps growing due to increased use of computers at early ages.

These children tend to breathe in a shallow manner. They tend to have fine motor control over gross motor control at an early age. They authoritatively point their fingers. They need to develop kinesthetic sensibility and to connect with their entire bodies. Movement exploration will take a little longer with these children. Sometimes the teacher will have to show them how far they can reach because they lack a good awareness of extended limbs and extremities. Use phrases such as "How far can you reach?" "Think about…," and, "Find the most important part of the skill."

Naturalistic
The naturalist learns through nature and examples from nature. The children who love insects, dinosaurs, or jungle animals are all using their naturalistic learning styles. These are the children who find what is happening in the great outdoors much more interesting than what is happening inside the classroom. One can actually see them staring out the window at the clouds and the way the wind is blowing the treetops. Again, to become annoyed with them does no good. The wonders of nature need to be brought inside.

These children will love moving like a giant wave, like an octopus, or like the plants on the ocean floor. Images from nature will always work, even if the assignment is something abstract. Talk about the angles of a preying mantis's legs or how many legs different creatures have. Ask these children to demonstrate the energy of a blue whale whose heart beats eight times per minute, which they can do by breathing very slowly or pulsing like a giant heart every eight seconds, and then that of a mouse whose heart beats five hundred times per minute, which they can do by inhaling in short little breaths while scurrying and darting about.

How to Use This Book

The book begins with a chapter containing exercises in which children can physically, in gross motor format, create the simple shapes that comprise the alphabet. The book's content becomes progressively more exacting and complex, ending in a unit on math and science, in which children enact division and multiplication problems in the concrete, physical world before they are asked to understand these concepts abstractly. The organization of the book gives you many options. You can utilize the book in the order in which it is written, which will give you themes and units each lasting a week or more. There is more than one activity for every day of the year; however, you will find that children will have favorites that they will want to repeat now and then. Children need to practice a physical skill four to six times before becoming completely familiar with it. As an adult you may think that an activity has become monotonous, yet the students will be quite content to keep practicing it and exploring the possibilities. You can do activities from this book that coordinate with what the children need to learn or are studying in their class work. Alternatively, you can go randomly through the book, picking and choosing what is appropriate for your group, to lend constant variety and an element of surprise to the movement sessions. Remember that the recommended age ranges that are printed with each exercise are only suggestions. Children progress at different ages.

Throughout the book there are opportunities for improvisational work. Always allow children to expand on a movement concept as long as it is safe to do so. Remember that mirroring and partnering are always options. Successful improvisation depends on the children's level of comfort and freedom and also on the quality of ongoing directives given throughout the activity. For this reason I have often given directives that can be read aloud to the students. Since, in essence, two audiences are being educated, there are directives for both teacher and student. Of course, first learning the movements yourself so that you can teach them experientially is a wonderful option for some of you. However, even if you have little experience with movement-education experience or are unfamiliar with a skill, the book gives you the language with which to introduce that skill to children in a way that is developmentally appropriate, understandable, and achievable for them.

The second chapter contains a substantial section on stretching and relaxing. Flexibility has traditionally been a forgotten component of fitness, and every teacher knows how stiff a person can get after sitting at a desk for long periods of time.

The book contains many animal activities because they are so well loved by children. The animal unit, in the third chapter, is the first one in which locomotion is involved. These exercises can be done by moving down an aisle or around a group of desks. If the classroom is arranged in an asymmetrical design, designate a pathway and choose a trustworthy leader. The pathways can be marked with contact paper cut into shapes such as paw prints, the alphabet, or numbers. For safety purposes tell the children that they should be far enough away from one another that they cannot touch the person in front of them if they reach their arms out. "An arm's length away" will become a common phrase. If the children are practicing an exercise with a leg extended, especially behind them, where they have no field of vision (e.g., #116: Monkey with a Tail in the Air), it is best to have them go down the aisle one at a time to avoid collisions. If you have an area in the front of the classroom, use it as a stage for small groups of students to perform the exercises that require more space (designated with special icons; see below). If even more space is needed for a group exercise, moving rows of desks to the side can be a group physical activity. Also remember that this book can be taken to the playground and on field trips. I have several weather-worn experimental copies myself.

The section on animal walks is followed by sections on various types of human walks and character walks. These help children learn different types of movement and movement textures. The character walks will allow the students to feel comfortable being a bit dramatic, which in turn will help to lead them into the pantomime unit, where they are called on to enact concrete and imaginary situations. To ensure safety, the book indicates when a preliminary skill is needed before a more advanced skill is attempted so the students will never be asked to do a skill that is beyond their ability. For instance, in the animal activity section, Seal Support (#112) comes before Hungry Seal (#113) because the children must be competent in supporting their torsos with their arms before they are asked to do the push-ups required in the more advanced exercise.

The third chapter also contains a long movement adventure, in which the children get to employ everything they have learned so far as they narrate a story. The movement adventure culminates in the game "Looking for an Elephant," an eight-minute cardiovascular activity. It can be broken down into individual verses or you can build up to doing the entire piece.

The sections teaching sports moves are rather lengthy because so many children receive physical education only once or twice a week. By leading them in these activities, all of which are broken down into achievable parts, you, as their teacher, can help them develop some sports skills. In the activities that involve specific skills, always allow the children to experiment with which arm, leg, or side is their dominant one for that particular move. Fine and gross motor control do not always coincide. In fact, given the choice, children usually choose one side for fine motor and the other side for gross motor dominance. This combination, referred to as crossed variance, has become the norm.

The gymnastics units are also sizable because of their physical and intellectual value. The physical value obviously lies in the development of strength, balance, and flexibility that is fostered with these activities. However, the intellectual value sometimes goes unnoticed. The learning of skills that can be done backwards, sideways, and inverted is valuable to premath, prereading, and writing.

The sections on holds, supports, and balances are wonderful for the development of control. Most children will agree that it is much more fun for them to see how long they can hold still in a shape that they have made or in a balance or gymnastic support than it is sitting still in their desks. And the lessons of physical management and control will transfer to other areas of study. If you observe the need for children to develop stamina, make sure to include sessions in which the children see how many of certain kinds of jumps they can do in a row, and try to help them make weekly progress.

Key to the Icons Used in the Activities

To help you find activities suitable for a particular situation, each one is coded with symbols or icons that tell you some things about it at a glance:

- the appropriate age group
- the size of the group needed
- if the task is advanced
- if props are required
- if a large space is needed
- if the game requires students to possess skills learned in earlier activities
- if physical contact is or might be involved

These are explained in more detail below.

Suitability in terms of age. In general, the activities are designed for children in preschool through the middle of elementary school (approximately age nine). Note that the suggested age groups are listed in both the "List of Games" on page vi and following each section's name. Any exceptions are noted with the apropraite icon. Again, these are just suggestions; take into account the capabilities of your group.

= Preschool to mid-elementary

= Kindergarten to mid-elementary

= Early-elementary to mid-elementary

The size of the group needed. Most of the activities can be performed individually, but a few require pairs, small groups, or the whole class. Each section is marked with a group-size icon, and any exceptions are noted following the activity's name. The icons used to represent group size are as follows:

any size = The children play individually, so any size group can play

pairs = The children play in pairs

small groups = The children play in small groups of three or more

whole group = The whole class plays together

If a game is advanced. The more challenging activities are marked with the following icon:

= For advanced children

If a large space is needed. Almost all activities may be performed in a small space—next to desks or tables. However, a large space is ideal for some of the activities (e.g., up and down aisles or with desks pushed to the side). The few activities that require a larger amount of space are marked with the following icon:

= May require a larger space

If props are required. A few activities call for the use of items such as balloons. Activities requiring props are flagged with the following icon:

= Props needed

If the game requires students to possess skills learned in earlier activities. Most of the activities are designed to stand alone, but some require skills learned in earlier activities. These are designated with the following icon:

= Requires skills learned in earlier activities

404 Deskside Activities for Energetic Kids ... 15

If physical contact is or might be involved. Although a certain amount of bodily contact between students may be acceptable in certain environments, the following icon has been inserted at the top of the exercises that may involve anywhere from a small amount of contact to minor collisions. You can figure out in advance if the activity is suitable for your participants and/or environment.

= Physical contact likely

The Activities

Shape Recognition and Replication

Shape recognition and replication are two of the most important factors in developing the abilities to print, read, and write. Circles are usually the first shape to be identified by young children. Children see circles in faces, wheels, eyes, balls, clocks, coins, plates, bowls, and spoons. Thus, some of their very first interactions, toys, and tools involve circles. The circle is also the easiest shape to draw with different body parts.

With the exception of Body Circles (#9), most of these exercises can be done either sitting or standing, although standing allows for more range of motion. Shoulder circles come first for several reasons. Children naturally shrug their shoulders and are used to moving them, so it is an easy place to start. Shoulders also tend to become rounded and fall forward after long periods of sitting at a desk or computer. Doing shoulder circles can reenergize and realign children's spines. Wrists are next because they are used so much in printing, grounding papers, writing, and coloring. They get tense and tired. They need to be moved and loosened up. Compare the sizes of elbow circles to arm circles. Finger circles develop fine motor control and will therefore be very challenging for preschoolers and kindergarteners. Make it fun for them by adding the song "Where Is Thumbkin?" However, don't dwell on this exercise for so long that the little ones become frustrated. Foot and knee circles add the challenge of balancing on one leg.

The star exercises allow children to feel what it's like to place their body in a straight line. A standing star involves making vertical, horizontal, and diagonal lines, all of which are used in the alphabet. When doing standing stars, ask them if their legs are vertical or diagonal. When doing sitting stars, ask them if their arms are horizontal or diagonal.

Use this opportunity to help them gain muscular control. Ask them if their lines are straight. Tell them to squeeze the muscles above their knees and to tighten their tummy muscles. Have them sit up straight by trying to remove all the wrinkles from the front of their shirt.

The next section, making lines, involves extending the line from within the body (laterality) into space (directionality); it also involves having fun while lining up. It requires cooperation and group problem solving. Children will interact socially and find commonalities and differences by comparing heights and finding out each other's birthdays. Time each lineup and keep a record; for example, "It took you one minute and forty-five seconds to line up colors yesterday. Let's see if you can beat that record today!" This gives children a healthy approach to competition as they try to better their results with each turn.

The section on curves takes children from the concrete to the abstract. First have the young children draw a rainbow in the sky; use size comparisons, asking them to make the biggest and then the smallest rainbow possible. Then begin to talk about the shape of a rainbow and have them draw curves in the space with different body parts. This exercise is extremely helpful in developing the spatial and shape awareness needed for printing letters with curves.

The figure 8 will be the most complicated shape to draw with a body part. Doing so develops concentration, a sense of abstract patterning, and fluidity of movement. First drawing the figure 8 on a board may be helpful by allowing the children to see the movement pathway and then follow it with their bodies. Also, the teacher can face the class and mirror the movement for the students so they constantly have a reference. (Remember to tell the children to go to the right when you're going to the left, because everything will be reversed.) Drawing with the legs and knees is also very good for balance. One of the biggest benefits of these exercises is that they involve movements that cross the midline of the body, an action that many ADHD and ADD children are very hesitant to do. While simply performing a fun activity, they will be incorporating much right-brain/left-brain activity. The exercises also provide good practice for those who are ready to begin cursive writing.

Remind the children that the alphabet is simply combinations of shapes and lines. When making letters of the alphabet with their bodies, the children can vary the size and body position, e.g., "Make a huge 'X' with your body. Now get low and make an 'X' with your body." This chapter gradually reduces the size of the letters children are instructed to make, from body size down to hand-painted letters. Also try combining body parts, such as trying to write the alphabet with hands and feet at the same time.

Circles

Except as noted

1. Shoulder Circles

Have the children circle their shoulders. Tell them: *Roll your shoulders forward, upward, backward, and then downward. Feel the shoulders make a full circle. Now reverse the direction. Go back, up, forward, down.*

Ask them to count the rotations, to count by even and odd numbers, or, if they are learning multiplication, to count by multiples of threes, fives, etc.

2. Wrist Circles

First try this exercise sitting so that the wrists are easy to isolate. Say: *Draw circles with your hands by bending your wrists. Keeping your arms still, first circle your hands toward each other and toward the center of your body. Then circle them the opposite way, away from each other.*

3. Elbow Circles

Have the children stand and bend their elbows, placing their hands near their shoulders. Tell them: *Using your elbows, draw circles at the side of your body as big as you can. Start by moving the elbows forward in front of your body, then up, back, and down. Try to draw a full circle, especially when your elbow moves to the back. Then reverse. Go back, up, forward, down.*

Tell the students that only their elbows make the circle and not to let their shoulders move with their elbows.

4. Arm Circles

To compare sizes with the elbow circle, tell the children to straighten their arm and, with one hand, to draw huge circles at the side of their body. Talk about

Circles

how these circles are much larger than the elbow circles. Switch hands. Ask if one side is easier. Try to make them the same size on each side. Practice with the less flexible arm until its circle is just as big as the one made with the dominant arm. Have the children square their hips and shoulders (their headlights) to the wall and move only their arms.

5 Paint the Sky

Create elbow and then arm circles by first dipping elbows (and then hands) in the magic paint on the ground. Paint a red circle with the right elbow and a blue circle with the left. Then, mix the red and blue paint on the ground, and, with a hand, paint a larger purple circle in the sky with an arm circle. Paint another large circle with the other hand, and continue to do so until the sky is filled with circles of different sizes and colors.

6 Finger Circles

Draw circles in the air with each individual finger. Give the fingers names such as Thumbkin, Pointer, Middleman, Ringman, and Pinkie. Duets using both hands at once are fun and sometimes easier than moving the individual fingers on one hand. For instance, the rest of the fingers can be secured while both Pinkies take their turn. For a variation, try adding the song "Where Is Thumbkin?" Have each finger run away at the end of each verse.

7 Foot Circles

Have the children stand on the right foot. They dip their left toes in the magic paint and practice drawing the biggest circles possible with the left foot. Start by making circles in the outward direction. Have them switch feet and draw big outward circles with the right foot. Switch feet again and draw big inward circles. Place hands on hips or out to the side for balance. Keep shoulders and hips even and parallel to the floor for balance.

404 Deskside Activities for Energetic Kids ..

8 Knee Circles

Standing on the left foot with hands on hips, have the children draw circles with their right knees. Switch legs. Try the other side. Tell them to try to keep the standing leg straight. Then they can try bending it.

After they have tried both sides, ask them: *Which is easier for balance?*

9 Body Circles

Have the children stand up with legs together and knees bent. Placing hands on knees, circle the entire torso (body) to the right and then to the left.

Stars

Except as noted

10 Standing Star

Have the children stand with their feet at least as far apart as their shoulders. Tell them: *Keeping your arms and legs straight, make the shape of a star with your entire body. Stretch your points out as far as you can. What lines are vertical? Horizontal? Diagonal?*

11 Desk Star

Have the children make the shape of a star while sitting at their desks. Ask them: *Can you straighten your legs and arms diagonally?*

This will help the children learn to stretch while in their desks.

12 Foreign Star

Have the children make the shape of a star while sitting on the floor. They can do this by extending arms diagonally overhead while stretching legs apart with knees straight. Remind them to keep their spines straight rather than letting them round. In unison, count the points of the star, using the hands, feet, and head as the five points. Then ask if anyone can count the five points in another language. See how many languages they can count in (how many foreign stars they can create). Pretend you are stars overlooking a foreign land.

13 Floor Star

Have the children lie down to make a floor star. It doesn't matter if they choose to lie prone (on their stomachs) or supine (on their backs). Say to them: *Lift your star points up off the floor. Turn over and make a star on the other side. Lift your points up off the floor again. Which side is easier?*

This exercise is a great core strengthener.

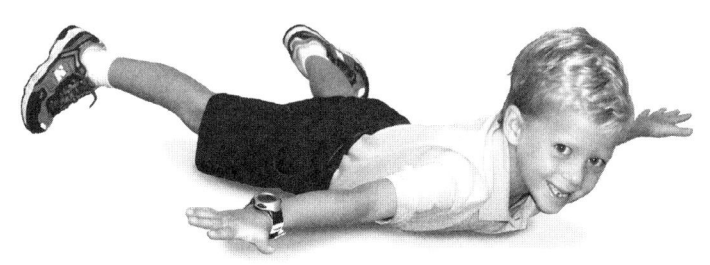

14 Sideward Star

While standing, tell the children: *Make a star shape while leaning to the side.*

Then have them lie down and make a star shape while lying on their sides.

Next, say: *See if you can balance on just one hand and one foot. Try each side. How long can you hold the star shape?*

15 Star in the Sky

Tell the children: *Put a star in the sky. Do a wide jump! Begin and end with your feet together.*

Lines

Except as noted — whole group

16 Birthday Line

Have the class line up in order of their birthdays as quickly as they can. Young groups may need to line up according to months only. Help the young ones review the order of the months.

17 Name Line

Have the class line up alphabetically by their first names. If the class is young and just learning how to spell their names, they can line up by the first initial of their names.

Have the class line up alphabetically by their last names.

Have the class line up alphabetically by their middle names.

18 Initials

Have each person in the class write down their initials. Then let them refer to and compare their initials. This is an exercise that includes progressive thought, comparative thought, and organization, as well as visual and audial processing and cooperation.

19 Shoe Line *(any size)*

Have the class line up according to shoe size.

20 Color Line

Have the group line up according to the color of the shirts they are wearing. Use the colors of the rainbow with black and white on the ends. Review ROY G BIV; if necessary, write it on the wall.

Curves
any size — Except as noted

21 Paint a Curve in the Sky

Tell the children: *Start with both arms straight down on one side of the body. Keeping both arms together, draw a giant curve in the sky, moving the arms out, up, and over to the other side.*

22 Paint a Rainbow

Say: *Every finger gets a different color to paint a huge rainbow in the sky, so dip your fingers in the magic paint on your desk. While seated at your desk, first try making a rainbow by lifting your arms up high. Now make a small rainbow by keeping your elbows on your desk. What is the smallest rainbow you can make?*

23 Big Rainbow

Say: *Now duck down beside your desk, and make a bigger rainbow by standing up tall and reaching your arms above your head. Finish by taking your rainbow back down to the floor.*

24 Group Rainbow

Try creating a group rainbow with the entire class. First see how the class would creatively problem-solve this one. Then use the following directive, if you wish: *Start with everyone in a close group crouching down on the floor with your arms down. Put yours hands in the magic paint and lift your arms up toward the sky, over in an arc, and then back down to the ground again.*

Then try a rainbow that fills the entire room. Have everyone move very slowly and in unison.

Figure 8s

Except as noted

25 Tiny 8s

Either sitting or standing, tell the children: *Let's see what the smallest figure 8 is that we can draw with our bodies. Let's start with our noses!*

26 Hand 8s

Have the children watch their hands for tracking purposes. Say: *Let's try some figure 8s with our hands in front of our faces. Switch hands. Then switch directions. Then switch hands again.*

27 Thumb 8s

Children will have the most fine motor control in their thumbs. Instruct them: *Try figure 8s with just one thumb. Start small in front of your face, and then make the 8s bigger and bigger until your are making the biggest figure 8 that you can across your whole body. Follow it with your eyes as you draw it.*

Figure 8s

28 Big 8s

This can be done solo or in a group. Tell them: *Make the biggest figure 8s that you can with both arms. Can you draw one that goes all the way across the room?*

29 Finger 8s

This is a wonderful exercise for fine motor control. Remember to be encouraging. Use the names of the fingers for fun. Say: *Now try figure 8s with just one finger on each hand. Start with the little finger first.*
   Then try with Ringman, etc.

30 Knee 8s

This is a progressive activity from drawing circles with knees (#8). Ask the children to stand up very straight. Tell them: *Stand on your left leg. Make figure 8s with your right knee while keeping your left leg straight. Now try with a bent left leg. Switch legs. Which way is easier: drawing figure 8s with a bent standing leg or a straight one?*
   This one is especially good for crossing the center line of the body.

31 Toe 8s

This is a progressive activity from drawing circles with feet (#7). Instruct the children: *Stand on one leg and keep the other leg straight out in front of you. Draw figure 8s with your big toe leading your leg. Now try it while bending the supporting leg. Draw 8s on the left and then on the right side of your body.*
   Then ask the children to switch legs.

32 Heel 8s

Say: *Stand on one leg and hold the other leg straight out in front of you. Flex the foot so that you can draw figure 8s in the air with your heel. Switch legs. Now try bending the working leg, the one that is painting. Now bend both legs. Try the other side.*

404 Deskside Activities for Energetic Kids ... 27

Alphabet Shapes

Except as noted

33 Diagonal

Have the children somehow make a diagonal line with their bodies. Then see if they can create two diagonal lines at once. Then three. Then a diagonal with another person.

34 Triangle

Have the children make a triangle with their bodies. The most typical shape will be a teepee or tent position with their hands and feet on the floor. Refer to that as an open triangle because of the open line on the floor. Then have them try to make a closed triangle. If they are having problems figuring it out, suggest the use of arms and legs.

35 Circle

Talk about how many circles there are in our bodies; e.g., eyes, heads. Tell the children to create a new circle with their bodies.

36 Body Alphabet

Standing up to begin, ask the class to see how many letters of the alphabet they can make with their bodies. Give a few examples, such as L, O, and M.

Alphabet Shapes

37 Foot Alphabet

While seated at their desks, have the students draw the alphabet with their feet.

38 Standing Letters

This is a progression from drawing circles with the feet (#7) and then making toe figure 8s (#31). Tell the children: *Standing, balance on one leg and draw the alphabet with your free foot. How far did you get before you had to put your foot down? Try the other foot. See if you can draw the entire alphabet without putting your foot down for balance.*

39 Partner Letters

Let the children see how many letters they can make with a partner.

40 Giant Letters

Have the children draw giant letters with an elbow. Tell them: *Reach as high as you can to make the top of the letters, and take the bottom of the letters all the way down to the floor.*

41 Hand-Painted Letters

Tell the children: *Make as many letters of the alphabet as you can with your hands as if you are painting them on an imaginary wall in front of you.*

Have the children paint giant letters at first so that the letters are as tall as they are. Then have the children gradually decrease the size of the letters until they are painting letters the size of their hands, and at that point have them change to a pencil grip with their hands.

Wake Up, Shake, Stretch, and Strengthen

The first section, "Shake Up," includes some fabulous activities for waking up. When children have been sitting very still for an extended amount of time, they may need to do some shaking. Use one of these exercises as a break after a test.

Isolating the head (activities #50–53) can also be very challenging and fun. These exercises will release tension from the head, neck, and upper back. This entire set of exercises can be done while seated.

When the children begin to look cramped or are slouching in their seats, they can wake up their spines and get their upright posture back with some supportive wall exercises (#46–49).

Sitting can actually compress the joints and make children feel tight and stiff. If these exercises are done repeatedly an improvement in the children's flexibility will become apparent.

These exercises can be refreshing breaks after a long writing or math session or after any session that requires intense concentration. They present an opportunity to teach terms such as "flex" (bend) and "extend" (straighten) to children who are unfamiliar with them. They also allow children to explore the use of joints such as the wrist, ankle, elbow, knee, and shoulder.

Shake Up

Except as noted

42 Hands

Have the children stand up beside their desks. Say to them: *Shake your hands up high, down low, out to the side, in front of you, and behind you. Now turn around in a circle while you shake your hands.*

43 Feet

Instruct the children: *Stand on your right foot and shake just your left foot. Then switch feet. Can you shake your foot while keeping your leg straight?*

44 Legs

Say: *Balance on one leg while you shake the other. Shake it in front of you, out to the side, and then behind you. Switch to the other leg.*

45 Crazy Shakin'

Say: *Shake both of your elbows like a crazy chicken. Shake them to the front, to the side, and to the back.*

Then say: *On your hands and knees, shake like a wet dog that just got out of the lake.*

And finally: *Shake your arms, legs, and body all at once like a loose goose; then shake tight and small, like a guitar string.* (You're looking for a very loose shake and then a tight, contained shake.)

Wall Exercises

Except as noted

46 Wall Touch

Have the children stand against a wall, bend both knees slightly, and make their lower backs touch the wall by tightening and pulling up their abdominal muscles. (This is very good for the abdominal strength needed to maintain good posture.) Tell the children to think of lifting their belly buttons to their lower backs. Tell them to visualize all the parts of their backs touching the wall—the backs of their shoulders, the backs of their arms, their upper and middle back, their waists, and the backs of their hips.

47 Wall Sit

Tell the students to stand with their backs against the wall as they bend their knees until they are the shape of a chair. You can talk about a 90 degree angle or about how their thighs are "parallel," or level, with the floor and the ceiling. Have the children count as high as possible while holding this position. (This is a good thigh strengthener.)

48 Wall Push-Up

Instruct the children to stand with a very straight body and to reach their arms out straight in front of them to touch a wall. Have them lean in toward the wall, bending their arms until their noses almost touch the wall. They then straighten and bend their arms again. Count by twos, or say: *One, straighten, two, straighten,* etc.

32 ... 404 Deskside Activities for Energetic Kids

49 Diving Arms

Instruct the children, *"In the Wall Sit position [#47], clasp your hands together overhead with bent arms. Keep your elbows in contact with the wall and your hands clasped as you straighten your arms."* Tell the children that this is the arm position divers try to maintain in order to go into the water without creating a splash.

Wake Up, Stretch, and Relax

Except as noted

50 Yes/No

When children engage in isolated head movements they stretch and relax their necks, shoulders, and upper backs. Start by asking questions such as: *What can your head do? It can say "yes" (nod your head) or "no" (turn it from side to side). Your head can help you look all the way up to the sky (look up) or all the way down to the ground (look down). It can help you look right or left. Look all the way over your right shoulder. Now look all the way over your left shoulder.*

51 Pigeon

Tell the children: *Move your head forward and backward. Keep the top of your head flat. Now try to be a sideward pigeon. Move your head to the side while keeping the top of your head flat. Pretend you are trying to hear what your neighbor is saying. Now try to hear what your neighbor to the other side is saying.*

52 Giraffe Necks

Say: *Try to hear what your shoulder is saying. Keep your shoulders down but try to make your ear touch your shoulder. Then switch sides.*

404 Deskside Activities for Energetic Kids ... 33

Wake Up, Stretch, and Relax

53 Diamonds and Ovals

Say: *Now make a diamond pattern with your head: Move your head to the front, the side, the back, and then the other side, keeping the top of your head and your chin flat as you go. You are making the corners of a diamond. Then change directions.*

Then say: *Change the diamond pattern to a circle or oval by making the movement smooth and continuous.*

54 Wrist Stretches

This one is good especially after printing or writing work. Sitting or standing, tell the students: *Flex your wrists as far back as you can by opening one hand and pressing the fingers of the other hand against the palm of the open one. Then try to stretch your wrist as far forward as you can by pressing on the back of the hand with the fingers pointing downward.*

55 Turtle Heads (Wrist Movement)

Have the children bend their arms, put their elbows on their desks with palms facing each other, and make fists. First the children will twist their wrists to the inside (toward the torso) and then to the outside (away from the torso).

56 Motorcycle Hands

A good vertical wrist exercise involves having the children pretend they are driving a motorcycle. Have them hold the handles and pretend to rev their engines and then reverse the action to slow down their speed. Take them through a pretend ride, having them lean into turns and go up and down hills.

57 Drummers

Have the children make fists with both hands with their thumbs facing the ceiling. Elbows are slightly bent. Keeping their wrists loose, have them move their fists up and down as if they are drumming, first emphatically and with a steady beat. Then they can alternate hands. For dexterity, proceed to double or triple beats with each hand. Lastly they can try simple rhythms like "1, 2, 3, hold, 1, 2, 3, hold."

58. Fruit Un-Roll-Ups

Have the children make fists, rotating their arms until palms are facing the ceiling. Tell them: *Unroll your fruit roll-ups as slowly as you can.*

They slowly straighten out their fingers while their fingertips slide along their palms, as if they're unrolling something that has been tightly wrapped. Finally, their fingers should extend downward and backward toward their torsos.

59. Pizza Platters

Have the students bend their arms until their hands are at their shoulders. Tell them they are holding giant platters of pizza, so they should keep their hands flexed and fingers spread, like a waiter carrying a big tray. Say: *Make your pizzas do the twist by twisting your flexed hands back and forth. Keep your pizzas facing the ceiling so they don't fall off.*

Note: This is a good exercise for the muscles of the hand and the forearm.

60. Spider Story

This is a fun vacation for tired wrists and fingers. Pantomime unzipping a breast pocket as you tell the students to unzip their magic shirt pockets and take out their magic spiders. Next, with both hands on the desk, "walk" the fingers toward each other and talk about how two spiders were walking down the street when they accidentally bumped into each other. They shake hands (shaking hands) and said, "Excuse me" to one another. "Oh," said one, "would you like to dance?" So, they did the waltz (holding hands, swing them gently from side to side). Then they did the twist (twisting fists). They also did the tango (palm to palm with 180 degree turns). Then they did break dancing (flipping hands from front to back on desktop) and then ran away (running with fingers around to your back).

Wake Up, Stretch, and Relax

61 Pencils and Erasers

If you're working with younger ones, have their flexed feet become erasers and their pointed feet become pencil points. Say: *Sitting at your desk (or on the floor), lift your toes up to the sky, flexing your feet as far back toward your hips as you can, reaching forward with your heels. Then, point your toes, straightening your feet and toes as far forward and as far away from your hips as you can.*

62 Flex and Point Balance

Tell the children: *Stand on your right foot and lift your left leg out in front of you. Be sure to keep your hips level. Keep your left leg straight while you flex and point your left foot ten times. Then switch standing legs.*

63 Windshield-Wiper Feet

With the children sitting at their desks, have them straighten their legs so their feet are lifted slightly off the floor. They then flex their feet and move them back and forth under their desks like windshield wipers. Begin slowly. Say: *It's a drizzle. Put your windshield wipers on slow. It's raining a little harder. Turn up the windshield wipers. It's raining hard. Put the wipers on the fast speed.*

64 Puzzle Feet

Tell the children that their feet have three parts that fit together like a puzzle: the toes, the ball of the foot, and the heel. Sitting, they first lift their heels off the floor; then they point their feet until only their toes are touching the floor. Then they bring the balls of their feet back down to the floor, and then their heels. They can continue to articulate through the foot while saying, "Heel, ball, toe; toe, ball, heel."

65 Piano Toes

Try to isolate the toes by lifting them off of the floor one at a time. Give the toes numbers: Pinkie is number five and big toe is number one. While lifting each toe

Wake Up, Stretch, and Relax

in turn, count along: "Five, four, three, two, one," then, "One, two, three, four, five." This exercise is sure to bring a smile and a giggle to everyone.

66 Foot Bridges

Foot bridges are especially good for children with pronated feet or fallen arches. Start by standing. Say: *Roll your weight to the insides of the feet, to the outsides, and then to the center. Find the bridge between your big toe and the inside of your heel. Use the muscles there to lift that bridge up. Do one hundred foot bridges! The only rule is that you do not lift your big toes off the floor or roll your weight completely to the outsides of your feet.*

This can also be done sitting. Once the children have seen what their feet are supposed to do, they can practice it at their desks.

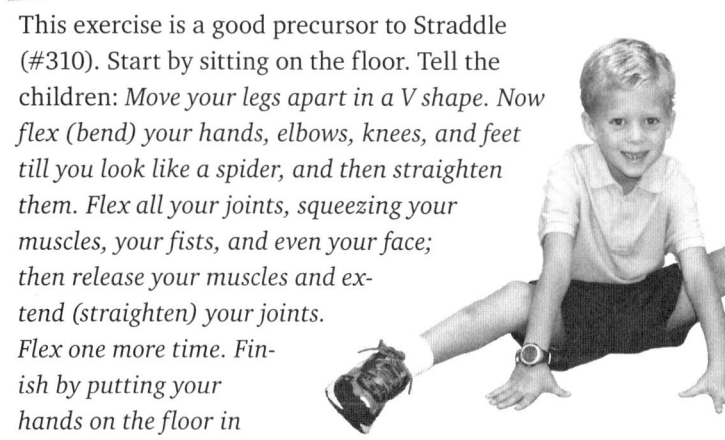

67 Giant Spider

This exercise is a good precursor to Straddle (#310). Start by sitting on the floor. Tell the children: *Move your legs apart in a V shape. Now flex (bend) your hands, elbows, knees, and feet till you look like a spider, and then straighten them. Flex all your joints, squeezing your muscles, your fists, and even your face; then release your muscles and extend (straighten) your joints. Flex one more time. Finish by putting your hands on the floor in front of your knees.*

68 Cat Stretch

Tell the children: *Get on all fours (hands and knees). Arch and round your back like a cat. First imagine stretching your belly toward the floor while keeping arms and legs straight. Look up at the ceiling so the top of your head points toward your*

404 Deskside Activities for Energetic Kids ... 37

Wake Up, Stretch, and Relax

tailbone. This causes your back to arch. Now round your back so that your spine lifts toward the ceiling. At the same time, tuck your chin so you're looking toward your belly button.

Note: This is a good exercise for stretching the back and increasing circulation throughout the torso.

69 Rubber Band

Start sitting or standing. Say: *Stretch like a rubber band.*
   Let the class interpret this one. Their bodies will stretch as they need to.

70 Neck Stretch

Ask the children to sit up very tall. Tell them: *Place your right hand on your right shoulder. Place your left hand on the right side of your head. Gently tilt your head to the left. Keep your shoulders down. Then switch sides.*

71 Elephant Ears (Arms and Shoulders)

When you see that children are sinking down or rounding forward in their seats you can help them stretch their chests and shoulders. Tell them: *Let's make elephant ears. Clasp your hands behind your head. Pull your elbows back and hold. Keep your chin and chest lifted. Release your arms and relax the stretch. Then make your ears again.*

72 Scratch Your Back

To increase flexibility in the shoulders, open the chest, and counteract slouching and rounding of the back, tell the students: *Raise one arm overhead. Now bend the elbow and reach as far downward as you can while scratching your upper back. Switch arms and do the same thing on the other side. Now bend your arm behind your waist to scratch your lower back. Switch arms to do the other side. Now try to make your hands meet by taking one over the shoulder and the other behind your waist. Switch sides.*

Wake Up, Stretch, and Relax

73 Straight Arms

To stretch the pectoralis (chest) and deltoid (shoulder) muscles, tell children: *Lift straight arms above your head and clasp your hands together. Keep your shoulders down. Now turn your hands inside out so that your palms face upward toward the ceiling. Pull your arms backwards.*

74 Calves and Backs of Legs

To stretch the calves and hamstrings and to strengthen the quads while seated, tell the children: *Flex your feet, straighten your legs, and lift your heels up off the floor. Hold for thirty seconds.*

75 Side Stretch

To do a side stretch while sitting at the desk, instruct the children: *Lift your right arm up next to your ear, and reach upward and diagonally to the left to stretch your right side. Hold onto your desk seat with your left arm for support. Switch sides. Now try this one standing up; lean on your desk for support.*

76 Hamstring Stretch

Have the students stand up facing their desks. Challenge them to put a foot on the seat of their desk and then to straighten that leg. Say: *Now keep your leg straight while you lean forward with a straight back.*

This will stretch the back, the hips, and the back of the leg.

77 Achilles Stretch

In the Wall Push-Up position (#48), have the children keep their heels on the floor for a good Achilles tendon stretch. Say: *For a bigger stretch, reach one leg further back, keep your heel on the floor, and let the front leg bend. Change legs.*

Hold for at least twenty seconds on each leg.

78 Shoulder Stretch

Stand with your side toward the wall (use the term "perpendicular" for older students). Tell the children: *Lift the arm that is next to the wall and place your hand on the wall. With your arm straight, slowly turn away from the wall, keeping your fingertips on the wall.*

This is a good stretch for the shoulder, deltoid, and pectoral muscles.

79 Square Stretch

Tell the children to stand next to their desks or a wall. If using their desks, they rest their hands and forearms on the desktop. If standing next to a wall they press the palms of their hands against the wall at hip level, fingertips pointing upward. Next they make the shape of a square by bending forward at the hip and stepping backward as necessary to create a flat tabletop with their backs. Arms are straight. The goal is to make a horizontal line with their torsos and arms.
Instruct them to keep their legs straight and vertical in order to create a good stretch for the back, shoulders, and backs of the legs. They should squeeze their knees together and press their shoulders toward the floor.

80 Foot and Ankle Stretch

We rarely stretch the top of the foot; however, you can tell the children that there are twenty-two bones in each foot wanting a little more space. Say: *Stand on one foot, and arch the ankle of the free foot so that the top of the foot or shoe is touching the floor slightly behind you. Bend the standing leg until you can feel a stretch in the top of your foot and ankle. Hold and balance for as long as you can. Change sides.*

81 Teepee

For an excellent stretch of the feet, ankles, legs, and back, have the students get on their hands and knees beside their desks. Tell them: *Straighten your legs, pushing up until your arms are straight and your legs are almost straight, resting on the tops of your feet now instead of your knees. Now bend your knees again slightly, but stay on the tops of your feet. Still staying on the tops of your feet, straighten your legs again. Find the place that stretches your arches the most.*

82 Wake Up, Go to Sleep

When students seem to be getting sleepy or before starting a new subject, have them put their heads down on their desks. When you say, "Wake up," the students lift their heads and stretch their arms, shoulders, and upper backs as if stretching after a nap. Then tell them to go back to sleep. Do this several times, making the stretches bigger each time.

83 Book Lifting

Before beginning a subject with a heavy book, have the children take the book out of their desk or pack and lift it up and down several times before beginning the lesson. See if you can add a lift a day.

84 Row Relay

Props: Dried beans or peas plus spoons or cups *OR* a book for each row of students

Dividing the class up into rows or teams can create new excitement and bonds. This exercise involves everyone, so it's great to use when there is a lack of participation in the classroom.

The rows can be the teams. The object is to pass a book or even dried beans or peas from student to student. (If passing dried beans, increase the challenge by using spoons or cups instead of hands.) Have the children pass the item(s) down the row and back up to the front where you can collect them. This entire relay can be done with the students sitting at their desks.

85 Toss and Answer

Props: Balloons

Balloons always wake up a class and can add fun to the naming of colors, shapes, states, capitals—almost any kind of recall work.

Throw a balloon up and have the children or a single child count, count in multiples, or recite a multiplication table as high as they can before the balloon touches the floor. The next student can continue where the other stopped. If the teacher or a designated student controls the balloon there is less chaos.

This can also be done as a partnered game where one student tosses a balloon in the air while another student names states, colors, counts in another language, etc., before the balloon hits the floor. They can work as a team and the teacher can record all the scores on a board.

86 Desk Dominoes

Have the person at the front of the row stand and leave his desk; then the person behind him stands up and moves to the front person's desk, and so on until everyone has stood up and sat down in the seat in front of them, with the exception of the first person, who has gone to the last desk. Then reverse the process. This could also be done with the rows as teams, playing to see which team finishes first.

Creativity with the Body

Children's naturalistic learning styles will shine through as they walk like their favorite creatures. This is a wonderful unit in which they can begin to discern between straight and bent arms and legs, weight placement, and tempo (e.g., "Does a rabbit move fast or slowly?" "Does a cat have heavy or light feet?").

Allow young children to contribute new animal walks of their own. Characterize each new walk and use the opportunity for comparative thought by asking how each new walk differs from that of other, similar animal walks.

Allow older children to show their artistic side with these assignments. Tell them to become just the jaws of the lion or just the tail of the whale. Another possible assignment for older children is to become a nonspecific, made-up creature. Have each child give his creature individual characteristics (e.g., is it amphibious, does it fly, does it float, how many legs does it have?).

The transition from replicating an animal to performing different types of walks begins to take children from the concrete to the abstract. The section on walks involves concrete, real-life pantomime situations and then imaginary ones (such as being inside a cloud), which will help them extend beyond themselves dramatically as well as in movement.

Learning different types of walks will also help children with the pantomime section. Pantomiming is fun for teachers as well, both because it is very entertaining and because it allows the students to become imaginary characters, permitting them to feel free to make movement and theatrical discoveries. Students will find out how much or how little force a movement requires, how exacting the placement of body parts must be, and how much facial expression may be required to portray certain images. They will also learn in a hands-on fashion how to make certain movements (i.e., wringing, washing, ironing, smoothing out the bed covers, etc.).

Both "Pantomime" and "Imagine" are units that allow children to develop their performance abilities. Initially, always have them practice together. Ask if someone wants to perform a solo while the rest of the group watches. Sometimes dividing the class into two groups will help in the development of performance skills and courteous audience behavior. It is always a good idea to pick out some outstanding performances to showcase to the rest of the class.

Activities from the "Finger Animals" section are appropriate to include when children are practicing their printing and writing handgrips. Creating finger animals helps to improve dexterity, relaxes the hand and fingers, and breaks up the monotony of practicing or learning the pencil grip. Have the children practice on both hands for ambidexterity and also to see if anyone might need to switch hands in their pencil grip.

Finger animals can also be done as shadow art and play if suitable lighting exists in the classroom.

The unit "Movement Adventure" is written as an interactive narrative of creative movement. It can extend over many days as the class goes in search of an elephant. Teachers should act out the activities with the children so they have an example to follow or improvise on. Teachers can even create a blackboard or storyboard of the adventure. The search for the elephant, which takes the children to the African savannah, into the jungle, down a river, out to sea, under the sea, and to the moon, can be done before or after a geography or science lesson. The adventure builds up to the activity Looking for an Elephant (#218), a simple and fun cardio workout done to the tune or rhythm of "Going on a Lion Hunt." At the end of the journey, have the children find the elephant in their imaginations (#219). This visualization process can be used again and again in the classroom as a relaxation technique. The students can imagine themselves doing well in the classroom, on tests, and in sports activities.

In the unit "Shapes and Statues," tell the children they can think of themselves as just shapes or as the shapes they can make with their bodies. For instance, have them see how many triangles they can make with their hands, arms, and legs. Then have them make a triangle with their entire body. Since the success of improvisation relies on how comfortable and free the children are and on the quality of directives from the teacher, most of this chapter is written in the form of directives to the students. It begins with the direct approach and then evolves into exploration and guided discovery. Continue to give directives, asking questions and making suggestions throughout the session. This will augment the session and will help to guide children in the development of their improvisational skills. Having the children make their own shapes and then having them teach one or more shapes to a partner or partners can also augment the exercises.

This is one of the most creative chapters and truly allows the children to make their own works of art.

Animal Activities

Except as noted

87 Elephant

Start with what is probably the most popular animal with children. Have them stand up next to their desks. Tell them: *Round your upper back, drop your head down between straight arms, and clasp your hands together for the trunk. Walk, shifting your weight from side to side as if you weighed several tons.*

88 Penguin

Have the children stand and think about what shape penguins are. Ask: *Do they look like they have knees or necks? Waddle back and forth on your heels. Use straight arms at your sides for your wings. Lift your wings slightly as you go.*

89 Rabbit

Ask the children to stand and to think about the long legs of a jackrabbit. Say: *Lift your arms straight above your ears to make giant rabbit ears, and jump on two feet.*

90 Gorilla

Have the children stand up and think about the long arms of a gorilla reaching to the floor. Then have them bend their knees and make fists, placing their knuckles on the floor outside of their feet. Say: *Stay low as you take tiny steps, shifting your weight from your knuckles to your feet.*

Animal Activities

91 Crab Walk

Have the children sit with bent legs and soles of feet on the floor. Say: *Place your hands behind you. Get up on your hands and feet by lifting your hips and torso. See if you can walk forward and backward. Crabs really do walk sideways!*

Ask: *Can your crab turn around in a circle? How about the other way? Keep your torso as flat as a table.*

92 Crab Push-Ups

Try this activity once they've succeeded at the Crab Walk (#91). Have the students get into the crab position, this time with fingertips pointed forward; make sure they can hold this position with their arms straight. Tell them: *Bend and straighten your arms, keeping hips high. Can you feel the muscles in the back of your arms working?*

93 Inchworm

Have the children stand up and roll down through their spines until their hands touch the floor directly in front of their feet. Say: *Walk your hands away from your feet with the tiniest steps possible. Then walk your feet back to your hands with the tiniest possible steps. Keep repeating these two actions.*

94 Birdstand

Ask the children to stand on one foot and place the other foot at the ankle, toes pointing downward. Tell them: *Shape your wings. Are they curved? Horizontal? Diagonal? How long can you balance? Now change feet.*

95 Duck Walk

Have the children stand up beside their desks and bend their knees as much as they can, allowing their heels to come off the floor. Tell the children: *Put your thumbs under your shoulders for your wings. Balance.*

Animal Activities

Walking in this position repeatedly across an entire gym floor is contraindicated because of the pressure it would put on the knees, but a few steps can be a lot of fun. Allow quacking!

96 Pigeon Walk

Have the children stand and make pigeon wings by pointing their arms downward and stretching them slightly behind their torsos. Say: *Walk around in a small circle, moving your head forward as you go. Try the other direction.*

97 Flamingo

Say to the students: *Stand up and make big wings with your arms straight out to the side. Balance on one leg, bringing the other foot all the way up to the knee of your standing leg. See how long you can balance.*

Although nonelimination contests are preferred, see who can stay in this position the longest. When someone comes out of the balance, have them start again immediately on the other leg. This is a great concentration exercise.

98 Sandpiper

With the children standing beside their desks, talk about how sandpipers run with very straight legs while taking dozens of fast, tiny steps. Say: *With straight arms held low at your sides (wings), run around in a tiny circle while staying way up high on your toes and keeping your legs straight. See how many steps you can take. Then try the other direction.*

99 Bunny Jump

Have the children tuck into a little ball like a bunny and hop, shifting their weight in very small, quick jumps from hands to feet, hands to feet. Have them say, "Hands, feet. Hands, feet. Hands, feet." Have the children hop around in a little circle beside their desks. Then have them go in the other direction.

Animal Activities

100 Bear Walk

Ask the children to get on all fours with straight legs. Tell them: *Walk on your hands and feet with straight arms and legs. Walk like a bear that is getting ready to go to sleep for the winter.*

101 Baby Bear Walk

Have the children get in the Bear Walk position with straight arms and legs (#100). Tell them, *"Shift all your weight onto both hands and then both feet. Hop your feet toward your hands, landing them outside of the hands."* This is very much like a bunny jump but with straight arms and legs; it is a good beginning exercise for upper body strength. The rhythm is "hands, feet (pause), hands, feet (pause)."

102 Camel Walk

Have the children stand up very tall and then round over until their hands touch the floor. Tell them: *Walk on your hands and feet, keeping your arms and legs straight and your back rounded.*

103 Roly-Poly Bug

Ask the children to lie down and pull their knees up to their chests. Say: *While on your back, curl up, grab your shins just below your knees, and roll from side to side.*

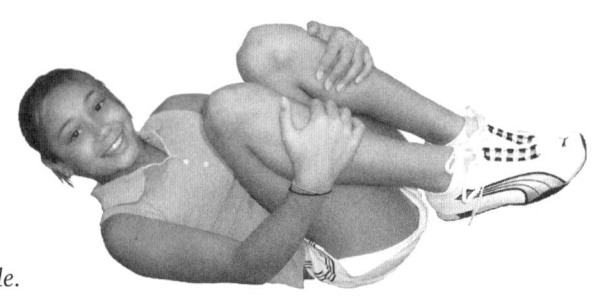

48 ... 404 Deskside Activities for Energetic Kids

Animal Activities

104 Caterpillar Roll

Have the children lie down prone (on their stomachs). Tell them: *Lift your arms up above your head, keep your body and legs straight, and roll across the floor.*

105 Jellyfish

Have the children lie down prone with arms and legs stretched outward. Say: *Lift your torso (body) off the floor and then release it. Repeat. This is how a jellyfish swims.*

106 Gator Walk

Have the children lie down prone. Tell them: *With your arms bent in close to your body, crawl on the river bottom. Keep your stomach close to the ground.*

107 Cat Leap

From a standing position, have the children push off from one leg, lifting one bent leg after another very quickly, as when a cat jumps; the rhythm is a quick "lift, lift, land, land." Have the children say, "Cat leap" or, "Knee, knee" as they learn this skill because the lift of the knees determines the height of the leap.

108 Wolf Stand

Have the children stand on one foot with the other leg reaching out to the side. Tell them: *Bend your standing leg all the way down, and place your hands on the floor on either side of that leg. Stretch the other leg out to the side and straighten it.*

Let them have fun growling and howling at the moon. Make sure they do both sides (this is a good stretch for the inner thighs).

404 Deskside Activities for Energetic Kids ... 49

Animal Activities

109 Cow Running

Have the children get on all fours (hands and feet) with straight legs. Tell them to run on their hands and feet, kicking their back legs out to the side. Say, *"Now try running around in a small circle; then go in the other direction."*

110 Horse Gallop

Have the children stand up with their weight shifted forward onto the balls of their feet. They can start at the back of each aisle and gallop one at a time to the front. Tell them: *Step "right left, right left," landing on the balls of your feet. Make it a quick "step step, step step." Lift your knees up high so they are bent in the air. Then turn around and start with the other foot so that the pattern goes "left right, left right."*

Now add claps, for "clapping horses," but first repeat the rhythm of the gallop by having the children clap it with their hands. Then add the legs. The rhythm is "quick *quick* (pause), quick *quick* (pause)."

111 Giraffe *Chassé* (sha-SAY)

Tell the children that the French word *chassé* means "chase." In a *chassé*, one foot chases the other in a step-together-step pattern, like giraffes loping across a grassy plain. When the legs come together in the air they straighten, whereas in a gallop the legs are bent. Start with the children all standing at the front of their row, and have them *chassé* down the aisle one at a time. Say: *Make a long neck by holding your arms up overhead. Make the head by placing one hand on top of the other.*

Have the children say, *"chassé"* rhythmically each time they perform the skill. Also tell them that their legs move apart/together as they go.

112 Seal Support

Have the children lie down prone. Tell them: *Put your hands under your shoulders and then push up so your arms are straight. Hold your stomach muscles tight for support. Take a few steps with your hands, keeping your arms completely straight. Don't let your legs or feet help you at all!*

Animal Activities

113 Hungry Seal

These are great modified push-ups. Say: *Hold your seal support with one arm, and draw a circle on the floor in front of you to dig a hole in the ice. Place your hand back on the ice, and bend both arms to reach down into the water to catch a fish with your mouth, the way seals do. Straighten your arms to bring the fish up out of the water. How many fish can you catch?*

114 Frog Jump

Have the children get out of their desks and bend their knees until their hands touch the floor. Tell them: *With hands between your bent legs, jump up and come right back down in the same position. Of course, you have to talk like a frog, too!*

115 Monkey Walk

Ask the children to stand up, and then tell them they can slouch. Say: *Bend your knees and round your back. Feel the weight of your arms drop from your shoulders. Now swing your arms from side to side as you walk in a circle. Then try the other direction.*

116 Monkey with a Tail in the Air

Have the children stand up. Tell them: *Place both hands and one foot on the floor. Lift one leg (your monkey tail) straight up in the air. Walk with two hands and one foot, keeping your tail up high. Then try the other leg for a tail.*

404 Deskside Activities for Energetic Kids ... 51

Animal Activities

117 Rhino Walk

Ask the children to stand and bend forward at the hips, flattening their backs like a tabletop. Say: *Make your tusk by cupping your hands on top of one another and curving your arms behind your head. Your elbows will be close to your ears. Walk in place with heavy steps. Are you walking on the river bottom? Can you run (in place) on the river bottom?*

118 Horse Kick

Stand with one foot in front of the other. Then bend the front leg until you can place both hands on the floor, shoulder width apart. Keep the back leg straight. Then shift weight to hands as you kick one foot at a time up behind you. Think of the rhythm as a quick "*kick kick (land).*" Start with the other leg next time. Keep switching legs.

119 Mule Kick

Make sure that everyone can do Horse Kicks (#118) first because this one is a little more challenging. Tell the students: *With both hands on the floor, keep your arms very straight and kick both feet up behind you.*

Have everyone let out a big "Hee-haw."

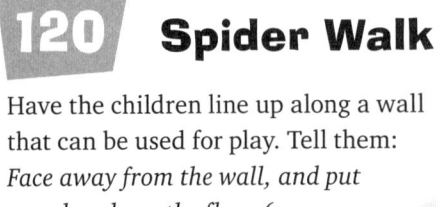

120 Spider Walk

Have the children line up along a wall that can be used for play. Tell them: *Face away from the wall, and put your hands on the floor (or ground) and your feet up on the wall. Using the wall for support, walk sideways with your hands on the floor and feet on the wall.*

52 ... 404 Deskside Activities for Energetic Kids

This exercise can also be done by having the children put their feet on the seats of their desks to see how far they can spider-walk around the desk.

Discovering how many different ways there are to walk is great fun. A tally can be kept on a board and added to daily as each new walk is learned. Individual students may want to contribute walks of their own. Describe each new addition, and, as you did with the animal walks, use the opportunity for comparative thought by asking how each new walk is different from previously learned, similar walks. By the end of the unit the class may have fifty different types of walks —one hundred if they include the animal walks in their repertoire.

Walks

Except as noted

* Simple Walks *

121 Low Walk/High Walk

These exercises are good for the quadriceps (thigh muscles) and the gastrocnemius (calf muscles). Have the children stand up. Say: *Find out how low you can walk. Bend your knees. Try to stay at one level. Walk past other people at this level. Shake hands and talk to each other.*

After a while say: *Now straighten your legs and walk way up high on your toes. Do not let your heels touch the floor. Try to touch the top of your head to the ceiling.*

122 Center Walk

This exercise can help children figure out if their feet have been supinating (rolling out) or pronating (rolling in and dropping the arch) and how to correct it. Ask the children to stand up. Tell them: *Walk on your heels, and then on the front of your feet. Now walk on the outsides of your feet, then the insides of your feet. Now find the center of your foot—it actually is located behind the center of your second toe. Try to put your weight there when you walk.*

Walks: Simple Walks

123 Toe-Ball-Heel Walk

Review the three moveable parts of the foot: the toes, the ball of the foot, and the heel. Tell the children: *First point the entire foot, and then flex the entire foot. Now try to walk, touching down one part of the foot at a time. Say, "Toe, ball, heel" as you walk, trying to step on each part as you say it. Then reverse the walk; try walking "heel, ball, toe; heel, ball, toe."*

Tell the children that divers walk "heel, ball, toe" on the diving board because the board slants forward, and dancers or people who are trying to walk softly walk "toe, ball, heel."

124 March

Have the students stand up next to their desks. Talk about marching—marching bands, soldiers, gymnasts, etc. Say: *March in place, lifting your knees. Do it fast, then slowly, then light, then strong.*

Tell them that gymnasts add the Toe-Ball-Heel Walk (#123) to their march. Now have them try a straight-leg march.

125 Peanut Butter

Have the children get out of their desks and assume any position they want to. Tell them: *Move as if you are stuck in a giant jar of peanut butter. How would you move your arms, your elbows, your hands? Could you lift your legs? Could you move your head?*

126 Weather Walk

Instruct the children as follows:

Walk as if you are caught in a light sprinkle, a rainstorm, a hailstorm.
Walk and move as if you are in the desert. How bright is the sun?
Walk as if you are in a blizzard. It is windy and snow is being blown at you.
Walk or try to move through knee-deep snow.
Walk or try to move through a windstorm. The wind is so strong that you have to hang on to something.

54 ... 404 Deskside Activities for Energetic Kids

Walks: Simple Walks

127 Head Walks

Ask the children to line up at the back of their rows. Say: *Walk as if the top of your head is leading you. Make sharp turns. Let it lead you in a circle.*

Then: *Walk as if you are being led by your nose (forward then slightly sideward, then to the other side).*

Then: *Move and walk as if your ear is leading you. What does it hear? Try listening with the other ear.*

Finally: *Stand up and then walk as if you are being led by your chin.*

128 Torso Walks

Have the children line up at the back of their rows. Tell them: *Lean and then walk as if you are being led by your stomach. Move and walk as if your hips are leading you everywhere you go. Can they decide where they want to go?*

Then: *Walk as if you are being led by your ribs. Start with the front of your ribcage, then get pulled from the side, then the other side. Now get pulled from the back of your ribcage.*

Then: *Walk as if you are being led by your lower back. Then by your upper back.*

129 Puppet Walks

Props (optional): A marionette

If possible, bring a marionette to class. Talk about how the marionette is moved by the strings pulling on its joints. Have the children stand. Instruct them: *Move as if your knees are leading you. Up, down, around, and sideways! Move as if your feet, knees, hands, and elbows all have strings attached to them.*

130 Arm and Shoulder Walks

Have the class line up at the end of a row. Say: *Lean and walk as if you are being led by your shoulders—one then the other. How about by both?*

Then: *Stand and then walk as if you are being led by your elbow.*

Then: *Walk as if your hand is leading you. Find someone to shake hands with, and then sit down.*

404 Deskside Activities for Energetic Kids ... 55

✻ Character Walks ✻

This section allows the children to become someone else, which can be a much-needed part of a child's day. Try one of the character walks, especially when a temperamental child is having a particularly tough day.

131 Toddler

Have the children stand and line up. Tell them: *Walk as if you are a one-year-old just learning to walk. Your head is big and heavy. Where are your arms?*

132 Wearing a Cast

Ask the class for some experiential knowledge on this one. Find out how many of them have worn a cast and what it felt like. Have the class stand up at the end of an aisle. Tell them: *Walk as if you have a cast on one foot, then the other. Walk as if one arm is in a cast. What about a cast on your leg so that you could not bend your knee? How would you walk if you had a cast on your back?*

133 Old Walk

Ask the class what they have noticed about how older people walk. Have them stand up. Say: *Walk as if you are very old. Your back may be tight. Your feet and ankles may be tight. Where are you looking when you walk? Are your shoulders forward or back? Is your back tall or rounded?*

It might be a motivator for good posture!

134 Emotional Walk

Ask your class if they have noticed whether or not they walk differently according to the way they feel. Have them line up at the end of an aisle. Tell them: *Walk as if you are happy, sad, worried, afraid, and then lost.*

Each walk can be practiced at least twice.

135 I'm Late!

Have the children stand up and try to walk quickly, as if they are late for class or an appointment. Say: *Walk as if you are in a hurry. Find the person you are trying to meet.*

136 Mad

This directive can be given as the children are still seated. They can try to portray anger both as they sit and as they stand up. Tell them: *Walk as if you are very angry. Other people are getting in your way. Find the person with whom you are angry.*

137 Look Out!

Ask the children how many of them have to cross a busy street on the way to school. Designate a walkway as a street. Have several students cross it at the same time. Say: *Walk as if you are crossing a busy street. Look in both directions. Go. Here comes a car from the other way.*

138 Waiting

Have the students stand up next to their desks or tables. Say: *Stand or walk as if you are waiting for someone who is very late. Pace back and forth looking for them. They are making you late for something very special. Are you looking at your watch? Are you looking for your friend? Impatient people sometimes change positions often.*

Pantomime

Except as noted

139 I'm Melting

Talk to your class about what things look like as they melt. Have them stand up very tall next to their tables or desks. Tell them: *Make the shape of an ice cube, and melt slowly. How slowly can you melt?*

Then: *Make the shape of an ice cream cone by standing up and crossing your legs. Make a big scoop by lifting both arms up overhead, rounded and with fingers touching. Slowly start to melt. Now make a double scoop of ice cream—each arm is a scoop. It is very hot outside and you start to melt until you melt all the way onto the floor.*

140 Popcorn

Have the children get out of their seats and crouch down low, close to the floor. Say: *Make the shape of a tiny kernel of corn on the ground. Begin to pop. Keep getting bigger with each pop until you are big all the way around.*

141 Tall Grass

Have the children stand up next to their desks. Instruct them: *Plant your feet on the ground. Wave like tall grass in the wind. Now get on your knees and try. What sound does grass make in the wind?*

142 Wave

Talk to the class about how a wave has two parts: the top that curves over and crashes, and then the undertow that pulls back. Have the group stand. Say:

Pantomime

Make your body move a like a wave on the ocean. See if you can make the top of a wave that moves forward, and an undertow that moves backward. Try a group wave that moves across the room.

143 Balloon

Have the children start in a tightly curled-up position on the floor. Tell them: *You are a balloon, flat with no air. Someone starts to put air in you so that you expand a little at a time until you are huge. Now float around the room.*

Then: *Now you are an inflated balloon, and someone lets the air out.*

144 Train

Have the children make a train all the way around the classroom. If physical contact is allowed, have them put their hands on the shoulders of the person in front of them.

145 Pretzel

Have the children stand. Say: *Make yourself into a pretzel by twisting and connecting body parts.*

Pantomime

146 Leaning Tower of Pisa

Have the children rise, and tell them they are going to Italy. Say: *Become the Leaning Tower of Pisa; keeping every muscle tight, lean as far as you can but don't fall down. Lean forward, sideways, backward, and then to the other side.*

147 Top

Have the class stand and ask them if they have seen a top. Tell them about how a top spins. Say: *You are a top balancing on the tiniest point possible, with feet together and up on your toes. Your arms are rounded overhead. Spin, but do not get out of control.*

148 Ocean Plants

This exercise should be done standing. Tell the children: *You are a plant on the ocean floor. Ground your feet (roots) on the ocean floor. Little waves move through you. Wave as a school of fish swims by. Move in slow motion. Floatingly move just one arm, then the other. Then move your whole body, with the exception of your roots (feet).*

Then: *Now get on your knees and try the same thing.*

149 Washing Machine

Twisting is a great way to wake up tired bodies. Do this from a standing position. Say: *You are a washing machine. Bend your arms and twist to wash the clothes slowly on gentle cycle, then fast.*

150 Egg Beater

Ask the children to rise because they are going to make a cake. Say: *You are an eggbeater. Your arms are the giant beaters. You are mixing a cake. Go all the way around the bowl. Now your legs are the beaters. Go all the way around the bowl.*

60 ... 404 Deskside Activities for Energetic Kids

151 Bouncing Ball

When the class is looking sleepy, have them get up and try this. Say: *You are a ball. Bounce; keep bouncing!*

Have the children think about how much space they use and the amount of force that is needed for each activity they pantomime.

Tasks
Except as noted

152 Rise and Shine

Ask the class what they do when they first open their eyes in the morning. They can begin as if asleep at their desks or lying down on the floor. Tell them: *You are just waking up. Get up out of bed, stretch, get some breakfast, sit down at the table, and eat.*

153 Bed

Ask the class how many of them make their beds or help to make their beds. The desk or table can be the bed. Say: *Make your bed. Pull up the sheet, fold it over, tuck it in. Pull up the covers. Fluff the pillows.*

154 Morning Activities

Ask the class what else they do in the morning before going to school. These activities could be done sitting down. Instruct them: *Brush your teeth, wash your face, and comb your hair. Does your mother do your hair? Show us how you look when that happens.*

155 Walk the Dog

Ask the class how many of them have pets and how many of them help to care for their pets. They can pantomime training, feeding, petting, brushing, or carrying a pet. Say: *Call your dog. Have him come to you. Put on his leash. Take him for a walk. He sees the squirrel and wants to chase it. Hold on to his leash!*

156 Doing Dishes

Ask the class if they have household chores. Tell them: *You are washing dishes. Rinse them. Dry them. Then put them away.*

Ask them if they have special ways in which they help their parents. Have them pantomime a way in which they help a family member.

157 Clothes

Have the class stand up. Then tell them it is laundry day. Say: *Take your clothes out of the dryer. Fold some of them. Iron some of them. Put them away. Some go in drawers. Hang up some of them.*

158 Clean the House

Have the class stand up. Tell them it is cleaning day. Say: *Sweep the floor, dust, vacuum, mop the floor.*

159 Picking Apples

Have the class stand. Have each student pantomime carrying a bushel or basket for picking apples and then putting it down where they are going to start picking. Tell them: *You are standing on the ground picking apples. Pick them by stretching up as tall as you can. When you can't reach any more apples, climb the tree to get the ones way up at the top. Hang with one arm, pick apples with the other, and toss them down to the ground or to your partner. When you're done, climb back down and pick up any apples that have fallen around the basket. Pick up that full bushel of apples and carry it home (back to your desk).*

160 Cooking

This activity should be done standing. Ask the students whether they help their parents with cooking. The children's desks can be their countertops and stoves. Tell them: *Prepare some type of food. For example, peel potatoes, cook them, and mash them, or peel apples and put them in a pie. See if the class can guess what you are making.*

161 Midnight Drink

Have the children pantomime being asleep in their beds. Tell them: *It's late at night. You wake up thirsty. You get out of bed to get a glass of water. Walk on your tiptoes (in place) so that you don't wake anyone up. Don't spill the water on your way back to your room.*

Imagine

Except as noted

162 Clouds

Ask the class what they think a cloud feels like. Find out how many of them have been in fog. Say: *Move as if you are inside a cloud. Is the cloud moving fast or slow? What kind of cloud are you—a soft, fluffy cloud or a thundercloud?*

163 Puddles

This activity can be done standing beside a desk or table. Say: *Jump over a puddle. Jump inside the puddle and splash all the water out.*

164 Picking Flowers

Ask the class if they have ever picked flowers. As they stand up, tell them they could be in a field or a forest and to show the rest of the class which one they are in. Say: *Imagine you are collecting flowers. Pick a flower and put it in your other hand or in a basket.*

165 Caged

Let the children choose the position from which they want to start. Tell them: *You are locked in a cage. Show us the walls of the cage. Try to get out. How tall is the cage?*

166 Kickboxer

Have the children stand in an area where they have enough room to kick. Say: *You are a kickboxer: kick, kick, punch, punch, jab, knee up.*

167 Ant

Watch ants work, if possible. Let each child assume his own position. Tell them: *You are an ant lifting a rock. Try hard. You need to push the rock off the hole of your nest.*

168 Reach for the Cookies

Have the children stand. Say: *You are reaching up to the cookie jar on the top shelf. Reach way up high for it: higher, higher, way up on your toes—oops! Here comes your mom. Sink down to your flat feet—sink down real low so that she doesn't see you at all. Now jump out to scare her, "Boo!"*

169 Strong Man

Have the children stand up and act as if they are very strong. Tell them: *You are a strong man lifting a heavy rock.*

170 Hands Up!

Let the children's desks be their counters. Say: *You are a bank teller going about your business. A robber comes in saying, "Hands up!" and demanding your money. You carefully take it from the drawer and give it to him as you push the alarm under the counter.*

171 Dinosaur

Ask the class to think about what kind of dinosaur each of them would want to be. Have each of them choose their position. Tell them: *You are a dinosaur. Show us what kind you are. Do you eat plants or meat? Are you tall or do you move close to the ground?*

Finger Animals

Except as noted

172 Turkey

Have the class start this exercise with their elbows on their tables. Tell them: *Spread the fingers of one hand wide for the tail. Make a fist with the other hand and place it against the tail. The thumb will face outward because it is the turkey's head.*

Finger Animals

173 Snail

Each child can make two snails. Starting with elbows on the tables helps to ground the forearms. Say: *Lift the pointer and the middle finger for the antennae. Wrap the thumb over the ring finger and little finger.*

174 Fish

Let each child's desk be the pond for the fish. Tell them: *Put your palms together and move your hands like a fish swimming. Make the fish use its tail.*

175 Clam

With the children sitting at their desks, have them put their palms together with the back of one hand resting against the desk. Say: *Open wide and snap shut. Now turn your hands over so that the other hand is on top. Make the smallest clam that you can (fingers together) and the largest clam that you can (fingers spread apart).*

This is a good wrist exercise.

176 Anteater

With the children sitting or standing, have them place their palms together. Tell them: *Point all fingers downward, and fold them together. Then extend your pointer fingers for the snout.*

177 Bird

This exercise can be done sitting or standing. One at a time the children can stand up to show the class how their bird flies. Tell them: *Put the tops of your thumbs (the sides with the thumbnails) together and flutter your other fingers like wings. How many different ways can you fly?*

178 Bat

Have the children sit to try this exercise. Say: *Hook your thumbs together to make the head of your bat. Then fly away with the rest of your fingers (wings). Can you make your bat hang upside down?*

This inversion is tricky but fun. The children may have to move their arms slightly to the side to invert the whole shape.

179 Chicken

Instruct the children: *Place your palms together and fingers in between each other with thumbs side to side. Keep your fingers straight. What do you call the thing on top of a chicken's head (comb)? Now open and close your two thumbs for the beak.*

Allow them to make sounds as they open and close the chicken's beak.

180 Two Deer Eating Leaves

This exercise can be done with elbows on the table. Tell the students: *Lift the pinkie and ring fingers to make the ears or antlers. Place the middle finger on top of the pointer finger. Open and close the deer's mouth by moving your thumb.*

The children may actually have to stretch their ring and pinkie fingers back in order to hold the position.

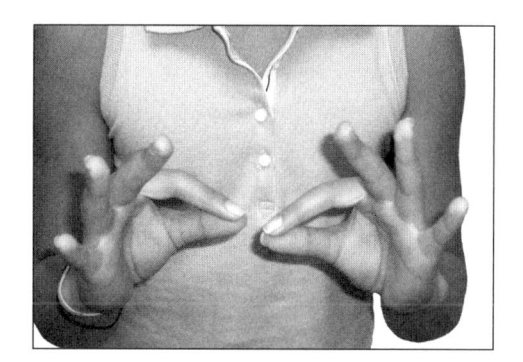

Movement Adventure

Except as noted

✻ Fly to Africa ✻

181 Fly to Africa

Begin from a standing position. Tell the class: *We're going to fly to Africa to find an elephant. Make an airplane: Spread your wings (stretch out your arms), start your engines (running in place), take off—up, up, and away (continue running in place). Look down and tell us what you see. Ocean? Land? What continent?*

182 Land the Airplane

While the students are flying (running in place), ask: *Does anyone see Africa? There it is! Go in for a landing (sink down to bent knees with arms outstretched).*

Then: *Crawl out of the airplane. Stretch up tall. Feel the ground. It is hot and sandy.*

183 Sunrise

With the children standing, say: *Look, we landed on the savannah where the sun is just coming up. Make a sunrise big enough for the entire continent of Africa. Make the largest circle you can, first reaching your hands all the way down to the*

68 ... 404 Deskside Activities for Energetic Kids

floor and then crossing your arms overhead as you stand up, then up and out in a circle back to the floor.

Trace the sun a couple of times.

184 Tall Grass in the Wind

With the children standing, say: *The tall grass in the savannah is swaying in the wind.*

Lunge (#319) back and forth sideways with arms overhead. Say: *What sound does the wind in the grass make?*

✻ **Wake Up** ✻

185 Sleepy Ostriches

With the children standing, say: *The animals on the savannah are just waking up. The ostriches were asleep with their heads in the sand.*

Round over, heads between straight arms with hands together on the ground.

Then: *They lift their heads up out of the sand, stand up, and open their wings.*

(The children roll up through their spines, lift their arms overhead, and then open their arms.)

Then: *They say, "Good morning" to each other. More ostriches wake up* (repeat movements), *lift their heads, open their wings, look up at the sky, look at each other, and say, "Good morning."*

404 Deskside Activities for Energetic Kids ... 69

Movement Adventure: Wake Up

186 Hungry Giraffes

The children are still standing. Tell them: *The giraffes are just waking up (raise straight arms together overhead to make a long neck; place hands on top of each other with wrists bent and fingertips pointing forward to make the head). They are hungry, so they eat some leaves from the trees above them (open and close hands to show the eating action). They are going to eat some leaves from the tree on the right and from the tree on the left.*

Mirror the children's movement (moving in the opposite direction as you stand facing them) to help the students learn right and left.

187 Flowers

Standing, say: *The flowers are just waking up. They are opening their big, bright petals up to the sky (lift arms overhead and open them wide, keeping them slightly curved). Try opening as slowly as possible and as big as possible.*

188 Seeds to Flowers

Still standing, say: *The seeds are growing in the soil. Let's start as a little seed. (Bending low, make the shape of a seed with fingertips together above the head.) Now pop through the soil (keeping hands together, extend arms overhead). Make a stem, and grow taller and taller until you become a huge flower and open your petals up to the sun.*

Slowly straighten legs to standing, stretching arms up and then open like a giant petal. Ask: *What color flower are you? Make another flower. What kind is that one? What color?*

189 Clouds

In a standing position, say: *The sun is so bright! Let's put some clouds in the sky (scooping and circling arms together in different places). Make some more and some more.*

Have the children make clouds of all shapes and sizes, high and low.

Movement Adventure: Wake Up

190 Rain

Still standing, say: *Uh-oh! We made too many clouds! Here comes the rain. Make a rainstorm!*

Tell the children to follow your lead. Start with your arms up high and brush your palms lightly against one another. As you begin to lower your arms start to clap softly. As your hands reach face level begin to clap loudly. Bend your knees and slap your hands on your knees. Keep bending your knees, and lower your hands all the way to the floor. Slap the floor. Keep telling the children that it's raining harder and harder. Finally, sit on the floor with the children and have everyone use their hands, legs, and feet to make the sound of a big thunder-and-lightning storm.

191 Tent

Still sitting, say: *It's raining so hard we need to make a tent. Get on your hands and feet. Keep your arms and legs straight and your hips up. Our tents are shaped like triangles. Is it still raining? Walk outside the tent (walking your hands forward). It is still raining—get back inside the tent!* (Walk hands back.)

Try this several times for great upper-body strength work.

192 Body Rap

In the tent position (#191), ask: *Do you see any African animals out there? Are they strange looking? You know, to them our bodies probably look pretty funny too. What do you think they are saying about our bodies right now? The giraffes and ostriches think we have short necks, and those four-legged animals are looking at our elbows and knees. The African animals are writing a rap about us.* (Stand up.) *Listen and repeat each line after me:*

Movement Adventure: Wake Up

Short necks, elbows, only two knees
   (pointing to each body part as you say it)
Human bodies are as strange as monkeys
   (swinging arms)
We've got waists and hips and fingernails
   (pointing and wiggling fingers)
Human bodies just don't have tails
   (twisting torso with hands on back of hips as if you had a tail)
Heads, our heads go up and down
   (pointing and looking up and down)
They go side to side and all around
   (looking to each side, then doing a half circle)
Our shoulders go up and down
   (lifting shoulders)
They go forward, back, and round and round
   (doing each shoulder movement)
We have noses, eyebrows, and big fat lips
   (pointing)
We have backs and sides that we use to twist
   (hands on sides while twisting torso)
We have two knees that we bend with ease
   (bending knees)
And now we'll show you our feet if you please
   (pointing at feet)
We have a heel and a toe and a heel and a toe
   (flexing and pointing foot)
Look at the funny way they go
   (shaking foot and circling ankle)
We have a heel and a toe and a heel and a toe
   (flexing and pointing other foot)
Look at the funny way they go
   (shaking foot and circling ankle)
Short necks, elbows, only two knees
   (pointing to each body part as you say it)
Human bodies are as strange as monkeys
   (swinging arms)
We've got waists and hips and fingernails
   (pointing and wiggling fingers)
Human bodies just don't have tails
   (twisting torso with hands on back of hips as if you had a tail)

Movement Adventure: Wake Up

193 Clear Sky

Still standing, say: *Oh, look! It's not raining anymore. Let's fill the sky with rainbows. Dip your fingers in the magic paint on the ground and make a curve with your arms from the ground, up and over the top, and back down to the ground again.*

194 Butterfly

Still standing, say: *Look at all the butterflies that came out after the rain. Make a butterfly by sitting on the floor, bending your knees and putting the bottoms of your feet together. Fly up high above the treetops (move your knees up and down). I see many beautiful birds in the trees. Let's count how many we see. Let's count in different languages.*

Lean over to stretch, reaching out with an arm and pointing to the birds as you count them. Talk about the other things you see on the ground as you hold the stretch.

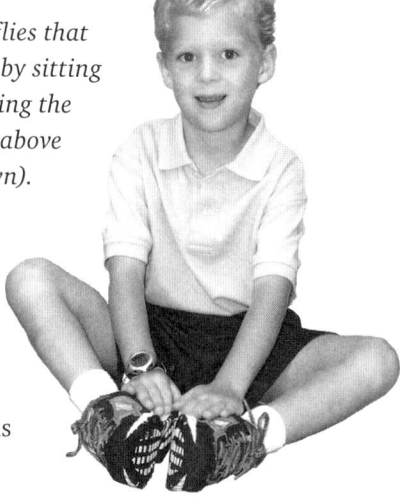

195 Put on the Brakes

Sitting in the butterfly position (#194), say: *Hey! Look at those huge jungle flowers! Let's land on them!*

To stop flying, bring your legs upright with knees together, grab your knees, and pull them to your chest while leaning back slightly. This is a good stretch for the lower back. Say: *Okay, put on the brakes!*

196 Flower Sit-Ups

While sitting on the floor, say: *Make a giant flower by putting your toes together in the center of a circle.*

If there is room, have the entire group put their toes together. Otherwise, make several flowers by putting several children together in smaller groups.

404 Deskside Activities for Energetic Kids ... **73**

Movement Adventure: Wake Up

Tell them: *Open up like the petals of a huge jungle flower by rolling backward onto your backs on the floor. But the flowers say, "Oh, no, not all those huge butterflies!" and they close their petals up tight.*

With arms extended in front of them, the children roll their backs up off the floor, returning to a sitting position. Keeping their backs round, they reach their fingers toward their toes to close the flower tight. Say: *The butterflies fly by, and the flowers open up again.*

Roll through spines back down to the floor again. Then say: *But soon the wind starts to blow and the flowers close back up.*

The children keep doing sit-ups with slightly bent legs to open and close the giant flowers as you narrate: *The wind stops blowing and the flowers open back up. But a swarm of bees attacks the flowers and they close up tight! The bees fly away and the flowers open back up. Then out of the jungle walks a monkey who wants to pick all the flowers, so they close up tight again. Then out of the jungle walks a zebra who just wants to smell the flowers, so they open up.*

197 Zebra

Although this activity could flow directly from the preceding one, it may also be done on its own. While sitting on the floor and reaching toward toes, tell the students: *The zebra has long white stripes.*

With your arms extended straight in front of you, point to one arm as if your arms are your white stripes. Then say: *And long black stripes,* and point to your outstretched legs. You're creating parallel horizontal lines or stripes with arms and legs.

Say: *Now take hold of your toes, ankles, shins, or knees. Your hands should stay where you have placed them for the rest of the activity. As the zebra, you can walk forward (inch forward on your bottom in a "walking" motion, keeping your arms straight and even* [use "parallel" if developmentally appropriate] *above your legs), sideways to the right (pivoting on your bottom, "walk" toward your right by moving legs in that direction), sideways to the left ("walk" toward your left), and even backwards (scooting backward on your bottom, one side at a time).*

198 Sandwich Sit-Ups

Sit on the floor and reach for or grab your toes (or shins or ankles). Say: *We should be getting very close to finding the elephant now that we are in the jungle. What do you think we should do with that elephant once we find him?*

Movement Adventure: Wake Up

Should we take him on a picnic? Well, if we are going on a picnic, we need to make some sandwiches. Open up like a big piece of bread (lying back on the floor). Spread some mayonnaise on the bread (sit up and pantomime spreading the mayo on your legs). Now close the sandwich tight (leaning forward, place torso and arms on top of legs). Oh, we forgot the cheese! Open the sandwich back up (rounding spine back down to the floor), add the cheese (sit up and pantomime putting a giant piece of cheese on your legs), and close the sandwich tight (leaning forward and extending torso and arms on top of legs). Oh, we forgot the tomatoes!

Keep adding ingredients, letting the children tell you what they want on their sandwiches. This is a great way to disguise sit-ups and to get many repetitions in!

199 Giant Sandwich

Standing up now, say: *What kind of sandwich do you think our elephant will want to eat? A peanut butter and jelly sandwich? Well, since we are in the jungle, we'll have to make that from scratch. You know where peanuts grow, don't you? In the ground. We'll have to dig them. Get your shovels!*

(Pantomime holding a shovel.)

First you find the peanuts and you dig 'em, dig 'em (digging motion)
You dig 'em, dig 'em, dig 'em (moving and speaking twice as fast)
Then you take the peanuts and you smash 'em, smash 'em, smash 'em
  (clapping and lunging side to side)
Then you find the berries and you pick 'em, pick 'em
  (reaching up high while lunging side to side)
You pick 'em, pick 'em, pick 'em (double time)
Then you take the berries and you smash 'em, smash 'em
  (pounding fists and lunging side to side)
You smash 'em, smash 'em, smash 'em (double time)
Then you take the sandwich and you spread it, spread it
  (sweeping reaches with parallel arms while lunging side to side)
You spread it, spread it, spread it (double time)
Then you take the sandwich and you fold it, fold it
  (bending over to fold yourself in half, hands to feet)
Fold it, fold it, fold it (sitting down and folding arms and torso over legs)
Then you take the sandwich and you cut it, cut it
  (slide edge of hand down center of body from nose to hips)
You cut it, cut it, cut it (spreading legs wide to make two pieces)

Movement Adventure: Wake Up

Then you take the sandwich and you eat it, eat it
   (moving hands from toes up the leg with "Pac-Man" motions)
You eat it, eat it, eat it (same motion on other leg)
Yummmmm (putting elbows on the floor)

200 Spider Sit-Ups

Sitting on the floor with legs apart like a spider and holding the stretch, say: *Wow! Making that giant sandwich was fun! There are a few crumbs left, but I see someone who might want those crumbs. He's not an ant. He has eight legs. That's right...a little spider. He looks so sad and lonely. Let's introduce him to Itsy Bitsy.*

The itsy bitsy spider climbed up the water spout (sit in a bent-leg straddle
   while reaching arms up high with "climbing" fingers)
Down came the rain and washed the spider out
   (reach arms down to the ground while fluttering fingers like the rain;
   then twist upper body like a washing machine, hands on ears)
Out came the sun (make a giant arm circle)
And dried up all the rain
   (reaching and patting legs and floor inside straddle)
Then the itsy bitsy spider went up the spout again
   (reaching arms and climbing fingers up high)

Sit-up Interlude (this is spoken):

Then a huge sleet storm washed him back down
   (rolling back to lie down on the floor)
But he climbed back up again (sit up, reaching up with arms)
Then a snowstorm washed him out (lying back down on the floor)
Keep naming types of storms that washed the spider out,
   lying back on the floor and sitting up again.

201 Jungle River

Sitting on the floor, tell the children: *Wow! We got washed all the way into the jungle river. Quick! Make a boat for Itsy Bitsy and us. Start rowing.*

The children get partners, sit with legs bent, facing one another and grasping wrists, and sing "Row, Row, Row Your Boat" as they lean forward and backward, rounding their backs to do partner sit-ups.

✳ **Out to Sea** ✳

202 A Sailor Went to Sea

This is a wonderful cooperation and coordination exercise. Still sitting on the floor, say: *Oh, my goodness! We have rowed all the way out to sea. Quick! Make a bigger boat. Make a big circle, but stay with your partner because we really need the buddy system out here.* (If the space is small, just keep the children in pairs.) *What do you see out here at sea? Here's what a sailor saw.*

Have partners stand (or sit) and face one another while saying the following rhyme and clapping hands together in rhythm. Pattern for each line goes: Clap own hands, criss-cross with partner, clap own hands, criss-cross with partner, clap own hands, clap with partner three times on *sea, sea, sea*.

A sail-or went to sea, sea, sea
To see what he could see, see, see
But all that he could see, see, see
Was the bottom of the deep blue sea, sea, sea

203 Jumping Sailor

For a second verse of "A Sailor Went to Sea," stand (if the children have been sitting) and add three jumps (along with the partner claps) while saying "Sea, sea, sea." This is sure to cause some giggles.

204 Jumping Criss-Cross Sailor

For a real coordination challenge, add a third verse in which the jumping pattern on "sea, sea, sea" goes: legs cross, apart, together.

205 Classroom Wave

Instruct the children: *Let's make a wave across the entire classroom to show how big the waves are out here on the ocean.*

404 Deskside Activities for Energetic Kids ... 77

Movement Adventure: Out to Sea

With children seated or standing, choose a path for the wave; for example, across the entire room, or row by row back and forth across the room.

206 Mer-People Workout

Standing, say: *Let's make our arms really strong so that we can swim around the ocean with the Mer-people.*

Have the class do bicep curls. Start with parallel arms extended horizontally to the front; then bend elbows so hands touch the shoulders; then open back out to horizontal. Do a few repetitions in this position. Then repeat with arms extended out to the sides at shoulder level, then overhead, with upper arms next to ears and palms facing back. Tell them: *To make it fun, let's count in halves each time we straighten and bend out to the side. 1, 1½, 2, 2½, 3, etc. Let's count in French when we take our arms above our heads. How about Spanish? Who knows how to count in another language?*

207 Sea Horses

Tell the children: *Let's kneel on both knees to make the tail of the sea horse with our lower legs, and curve our arms up overhead and forward to make the body and head of a sea horse.*

208 Sea Anemones

With the class sitting on the floor, ask: *Can you say "anemone"? Anemones open and close and open and close, then roll to another place.* Sit in a tuck position (#308) and then open arms and legs into a V-sit (#314).

Then say: *They close and open and close and roll to another place.* Roll like a roly-poly bug (#103).

"Then they open and close again and roll to another place, returning to a sitting position from which they can open and close again."

209 Sharks

Still sitting, say: *Let's be sharks!*

Have the children roll onto their sides. Tell them: *Balance completely on your side with your arms extended straight above your heads. Keep your legs turned out so just your heels, and not your toes, are touching to make the tail. Keeping your arms straight overhead, open and close your arms to make a giant shark mouth.*

210 Flying Fish

With the children still balancing on their sides, say: *Wow, look at all the sharks. It is getting scary here! Let's become flying fish and get away from all of the sharks!*

Kneel and then stand; place hands together overhead and "fly" up and out of the water, then above the water by lowering arms out to the side. Say: *Look at the water skier. Look at the big ships. What else do you see on the surface of the ocean?*

✳ To the Moon ✳

211 Rocket to the Moon

Standing with arms outstretched as if you're still flying fish, tell the children: *Every time our fish go back into the water the shark is still following us. Let's make a rocket to fly far away from here. Ready (place hands together overhead with straight arms), countdown: 10, 9, 8, 7, 6, 5, 4, 3, 2, 1, blastoff!*

212 Feeling Floaty

Standing as if floating in outer space, say: *Let's fly through outer space (improvise). What do you see? What continents? What planets? Let's land on the moon! Come in for a landing.*

213 Balance on the Moon

Standing, say: *Crawl out of your spaceship. What does the surface of the moon feel like? Let an arm float up. Let a leg float up. What does it feel like to be somewhere that has only one-sixth of the earth's gravity? Let's put the American flag on the moon. Balance on one leg to make the flagpole. Now, bend the other leg and lift that foot up to your knee to make the flag. Now extend your leg in front of you to make a bigger flag. Now, let's put our school's flag on the moon* (lower the first

Movement Adventure: To the Moon

leg, and lift and extend the other leg). *Now the state flag* (lift the first leg again, this time to the side). *Now a flag with an elephant on it. If there is an elephant here he might see the flag and come to it* (extend second leg to the side).

Continue with other flags, making different-colored flags if you run out of affiliation flags. Then say: *Choose your favorite way to balance and see how long you can hold it.*

214 Big Kicks on the Moon

With the children still standing, say: *Can you kick really high on the moon? Kick your right leg up to the front. Then your left. Now kick your right leg out to the side. Try to kick your left leg out to the side all the way up to your ear. Now kick to the back on the right. Now try to keep your chest up as you kick your left leg to the back.*

215 Tiptoe Around the Crater

Still standing, say: *Wow! Look at the big crater!* (Rise up on the balls of your feet like you're peering into the crater.) *Let's tiptoe around the edge of it. Hold your arms out for balance and tiptoe around in a circle.*

216 Jumps on the Moon

Still standing, say: *Let's see how high we can jump on the moon. Try to stay in the air as long as you can. Let's see how many jumps we can do on the moon. Now let's count by twos.*

217 Back to Earth

Still standing, tell the class: *Being on the moon is fun, but we still haven't found our elephant, and I don't think we will find him on the moon! We had better head back to the jungle on planet Earth to look for him. Let's take a little bit of moon dust with us. Put some in our pockets. Climb back into the spaceship and count down to blastoff.* (Extend arms overhead in a rocket shape.) *10, 9, 8, 7, 6, 5, 4, 3, 2, 1. Blastoff!* (Open arms out to the side.) *There is Saturn. There is Venus. There is Mars. And there is our home planet, earth. Look, there is the continent of Africa. Land there. Come in for an easy and soft landing.*

✻ Back on Earth ✻

218 Looking for an Elephant

Studies indicate that children need at least eight minutes of cardiovascular exercise each day. This game will provide it. Try one verse first. On subsequent days, add a chorus or a verse at a time until the children's fitness level has improved enough to allow them to do the whole song. The activity incorporates animal movements learned earlier in this chapter.

Say to the class, "Okay, everyone, make your elephant ears (holding hands by ears). Let's go! Repeat each line after me."

(To the tune or rhythm of "Going on a Lion Hunt")

Chorus:

Looking for an elephant   **Class:** *Looking for an elephant*
   (Marching in place, tilting side to side while holding ears)
I'm not afraid   **Class:** *I'm not afraid*
   (Jogging in place, thumbs to chest)
Marching through the jungle   **Class:** *Marching through the jungle*
   (Marching in place while pumping opposite arms)
Where the animals play   **Class:** *Where the animals play*
   (Kicking legs out side to side with arms also moving side to side)

Oh, look over there. There's a gate!
   (Bend knees and point)
Can't go over it   **Class:** *Can't go over it*
   (Lift each knee)
Can't go under it   **Class:** *Can't go under it*
   (Duck down)
Can't go around it   **Class:** *Can't go around it*
   (Turn in a circle)
Got to go through it   **Class:** *Got to go through it*
   (Pantomime going through a gate)
Let's call him: Elephant are you here?
   (Pantomime looking around)
No, but I see some frogs jumping
   (Jump from a low position; #114: Frog Jump)
And I see some bears walking through the forest
   (#100: Bear Walk)

Movement Adventure: Back on Earth

And I see some baby bears jumping from hands to feet
    (#101: Baby Bear Walk)
But no elephant. Come on. Let's try another direction. Let's go this way
    (Entire class faces in a new direction)

        (Repeat chorus with actions, this time saying,
        "Jogging through the jungle" instead of marching.)

Oh, look over there. There's a huge tree!
    (Bend knees and point)

Can't go over it	**Class:** *Can't go over it*
(Lift each knee)	
Can't go under it	**Class:** *Can't go under it*
(Duck down)	
Can't go around it	**Class:** *Can't go around it*
(Turn in a circle)	
Got to climb up it	**Class:** *Got to climb up it*

Come on! Let's climb the tree.
    (Pantomime climbing motions)
Let's call him: Elephant are you here?
    (Pantomime looking around)
No, but I see some chimps swinging in the trees
    (Big swinging motions with arms)
And I see some gorillas
    (Place weight on knuckles and feet with shoulders up; #90: Gorilla)
And I see some monkeys with tails in the air
    (Keeping weight on knuckles, lift one leg in the air; #116: Monkey with a Tail in the Air)
But no elephant. Come on, let's go this way
    (Facing another direction with hands at ears)

        (Repeat chorus with actions, this time saying,
        "Skipping through the jungle" instead of jogging.)

Oh, look over there. There's a bridge!
    (Bend knees and point)

Can't go over it	**Class:** *Can't go over it*
(Lift each knee)	
Can't go under it	**Class:** *Can't go under it*
(Duck down)	
Can't go around it	**Class:** *Can't go around it*
(Turn in a circle)	

Movement Adventure: Back on Earth

Got to go across it   **Class:** *Got to go across it*
Quickly! I don't know if it's safe!
    (Pantomime crossing a wobbly footbridge)
Let's call him: Elephant are you here?
    (Pantomime looking around)
No, but I see some flamingos down by the water
    (Spread arms wide and lift a leg with toe to knee; #97: Flamingo)
And I see some sandpipers taking fast, tiny steps
    (Run in very small circles on tiptoes with arms out; #98: Sandpiper)
But no elephant! Come on! Let's go this way!
    (Face another direction)

      (Repeat chorus with actions, this time saying,
        "Running through the jungle" instead of skipping.)

Oh, look over there. There's some grass!
    (Bend knees and point)
Can't go over it   **Class:** *Can't go over it*
    (Lift each knee)
Can't go under it   **Class:** *Can't go under it*
    (Duck down)
Can't go around it   **Class:** *Can't go around it*
    (Turn in a circle)
Got to go through it   **Class:** *Got to go through it*
Lift your legs up high. This grass is taller than we are!
    (Pantomime pushing your way through tall grass)
Let's call him: Elephant are you here?
    (Pantomime looking around)
No, but I see some giraffes chasséing through the grass
    (Make the neck and head with arms and hands up, then chassé with
    back leg chasing front leg; #111)
And I see some zebras galloping through the grass
    (Clap hands while doing a galloping rhythm with the feet)
And I see some ostriches taking long strides
    (Long, low runs or leaps)
But no elephant! Come on. Let's go this way!
    (Face another direction)

      (Repeat chorus with actions, this time saying,
        "Kicking through the jungle" instead of running.)

Oh, look over there. There's a cave!
    (Bend knees and point)

Can't go over it   **Class:** *Can't go over it*
    (Lift each knee)

Can't go under it   **Class:** *Can't go under it*
    (Duck down)

Can't go around it   **Class:** *Can't go around it*
    (Turn in a circle)

Got to go in it   **Class:** *Got to go in it*
    (Softly, creep into the cave)

Let's call him: Elephant are you here?
Oh, oh! We woke up a lion who was sleeping in here!
Quick! Run! (run in place)
Run like a lion! (run faster)
Run like a jaguar! (run faster)
Run like a cheetah! (run faster)
Quick, make your wings and let's fly home (arms out)
Up over the jungle, over Africa, across the ocean, back to the U.S.A., back to school, and back to your desks
    (Students return to sitting).

Finish with: *Close your eyes and think of all the places you've been. Think of all the movements you've done and all the animals you've seen. Now imagine the most magnificent elephant that you can, and know that you can always find him in your imagination.*

219 Relaxation Exercise

With the class now sitting, say: *Just as you imagined your elephant, imagine your favorite place. Close your eyes. Relax all of your muscles. Think of how you get to your favorite place. Is your elephant leading you there? Are you flying there on a magic carpet? Think of what the weather is like there. Is the sun shining? Think of the sounds that you hear. Are there birds singing in the air? Do you hear the ocean? Do you feel a breeze blowing around you? Think of all the colors in your favorite place. Then think of how happy you are in your favorite place. Keep all of those thoughts and feelings as you imagine yourself as the best student you can be. Think about how easy and relaxed you feel. Think of how happy that makes you. Now it is time to leave your special place. See yourself walking away but keep all of those feelings with you. Now open your eyes.*

Shapes and Statues

Except as noted

✻ Simple Shapes and Statues ✻

220 Famous Statues

Ask the children to think of their body as a statue and to stand or sit in that position. It's a good idea to start with a specific example of a well-known sculpture such as the Statue of Liberty or the Thinker. See how long they can hold the pose.

221 Everyday Shapes

Ask the children to stand. Have them make the shape of the Eiffel tower, a pear, a tree, a teepee, a house, a car, etc. Talk about how a tree is a tall shape and a house might be a rectangle. Talk about curves and angles that their shapes might have.

222 Make Your Favorite Shapes

Ask the children what their favorite shapes are. After they have picked their favorite shape, instruct them to try to make that shape with their bodies. Try this one again later after they have gained experience and confidence with this sort of activity. See if their favorite shape has changed. Perhaps they've discovered a new one.

223 Tall/Low Shapes

With the students standing, say: *Make a tall shape. Teach your shape to someone else. Mirror each other's shapes.*

404 Deskside Activities for Energetic Kids ... 85

Then say: *Now make a low shape close to the ground.*

After the children do that, say: *Now make your low shape and then your tall shape.*

224 Wide Shape

Have the class stand up and review their tall and low shapes. Tell them: *Make a wide shape, reaching out with your arms, legs, and every part of your body. Then do your tall shape. Then make your wide shape again.*

Talk to the children about an "a, b, a" structure in music, poetry, and art.

225 Round Shape

Ask the class to stand and review their previous shapes. Then let them know they do not have to be on their feet when they make this next shape. With the class sitting (or lying down), say: *Can you make a version of each of these shapes while sitting down (or while on your backs, etc.)? Sculpt a round shape. Then make your tall shape. Then your low shape. Then your wide shape.*

226 Square Shape

Have the children begin in a standing position and practice their previous shapes. Then say: *Carve a square shape with your body. How many edges can you make? Now make your round shape. Then your square shape. Then your round shape again.*

227 Angled Shape

Ask the children to stand. Say: *Make a shape with lots of angles, corners, and points. Can you mirror someone else's angled shape?*

Talk about how every object has legs or a base that supports it or on which it rests. Chairs and tables usually have four legs or bases, as do many animals. Shapes can have any number of bases.

228 Flat Shape

Ask the children to stand, and have them review their previous shapes. Next, tell them: *Make a flat shape. Then your tall shape. Then your low shape. Then your wide shape. Then your round shape. Then your square shape.*

229 Twisted Shape

Have the children stand, and let them know that they do not have to be on both feet for any given shape. Tell them: *Make a twisted shape—as twisted as you can get. Can you teach that shape to someone else?*

✳ Base of Support ✳

230 One Base

Have the class stand. Tell them: *Make a shape with one base of support.*

Give them examples, such as balancing on one leg, on one side, on your back, on your tummy, etc.

231 Two Bases

Still standing, say: *Make a shape with two bases of support. The bases do not have to be hands and feet! What other body parts can you use?*

232 One Hand, Two Feet

Say: *Make a shape with one hand and two feet on the floor. Put weight on your hand and your feet.*

233 Two Hands, One Leg

Then: *Make a shape with two hands and one foot or leg on the floor.*

234 Head, Hand, Foot

Then: *Create a shape with your head, one hand, and one foot on the floor.*

235 Elbows

Next: *Make a shape with your elbows touching the floor.*

236 Side

Then say: *Make a shape while balancing on your side. It can have one, two, three, or more bases. How many ways can you figure out how to do this?*

237 Twenty Bases

Finally: *Make a shape with twenty bases of support* (i.e., ten fingers and ten toes—this can serve as a riddle for the group to solve).

✻ Open and Closed Spaces ✻

238 Open Spaces

Tell the class: *Mold a shape with open spaces.*

If your students are old enough to understand, talk about positive and negative space in shapes. Next, say: *Then close the spaces in your shape. Then make another shape with open spaces. How many open spaces can you make with your body?*

239 Closed Spaces

Tell the class: *Make a shape with closed spaces (e.g., a car or a sleeping animal). Then open up a space. Then another. How many closed spaces can you make with your body that you later open up?*

240 Symmetry/Asymmetry

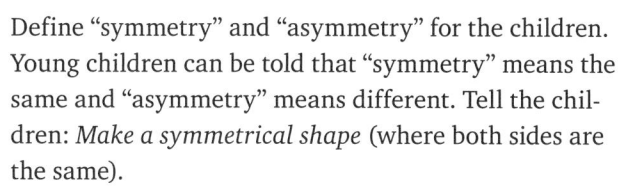

Define "symmetry" and "asymmetry" for the children. Young children can be told that "symmetry" means the same and "asymmetry" means different. Tell the children: *Make a symmetrical shape* (where both sides are the same).

Then ask them to: *Create an asymmetrical shape* (one with at least two different sides). An example of an asymmetrical shape is pictured on the right.

Kaleidoscope (Moving with Shapes)

241 Shape Pattern

Define the word "sequence." Then tell the children: *Create some of your own shapes. Choose three or four favorite shapes and perform them one after another. Repeat the sequence twice.*

This is a wonderful way in which to understand and learn sequencing.

242 Up-and-Down Shape

Instruct the students: *Choose a shape. Can your shape move up and down? Can your leg or legs bend and straighten? What parts can move up and down in your shape? Pretend that your shape is a machine that moves up and down. Go through your shape pattern and make each part of your shape move up and down.*

243 Forward/Backward Shape

Next, tell the class: *Make another shape that can move forward. Get a partner and together move your shapes forward in space.*

Shapes and Statues: Kaleidoscope (Moving with Shapes)

Make sure that the children maintain the integrity of their shapes. Tell them that we still want to be able to tell what shape they are in and that only a couple of parts should move.

Then ask: *Can your shape move backward?*

Note: To avoid collisions and to develop performance abilities, consider having demonstrations by individuals or one pair at a time.

244 Circular Floor Pattern

Tell the children: *This time make a shape that can turn around in a circle. Perhaps your shape has one part that stays in the center—like a foot or an elbow—while the rest moves around it.*

Introduce the word "pivot."

245 Machine Shape

Say: *Build a shape that has moveable parts in every direction, like a complicated machine. Perhaps an elbow moves in and out, a leg moves up and down, your head turns from side to side.*

246 Sideward Shape

Ask: *Can your shape move sideways? Can all the shapes within your big shape move to the right? To the left? Can just parts of your shape move out to the side and back to center?*

247 Mirror Shape

Tell the class to pair up into groups of two and stand near their partner. Say: *Have your partner make a shape. Mirror that shape exactly.*

After the first player has gone, have the partners switch roles.

Have the children repeat the sequence, building different shapes each time.

Shapes and Statues: Kaleidoscope (Moving with Shapes)

248 Inverted Shape

Tell the children that "inverted" means upside down. Have them stand up. Say: *Build a shape. Can you invert your shape or turn it upside down? Can you turn part of it upside down? Another part?*

249 Partner Shape

Tell the class: *Make a shape with a partner that could not exist without your partner. Maybe you need each other for balance. Open and close all the spaces.*

Then have them try with three people making a shape together. Find the moveable parts.

250 Shifting Shape

Make a group shape by playing add on. Start with one student. Add one person at a time so that the children study the sculpture and then make their contribution to it. Make a group shape. Have someone leave and add on somewhere else.

251 Jungle Gym

Make a group shape in which each child has to create as many open spaces as possible. Have one person at a time crawl through as many open spaces as they can and then add back on. It's a human jungle gym!

By this time children will be comfortable experiencing movement simply as textures, qualities, and styles. This section can be read directly to the children either in the command style or through exploration (e.g., "How can you dart? Can your nose dart?"). When these activities are given in the command style, it teaches children to listen carefully and process quickly so that they can respond immediately to the one-word instructions. The ordering of instructions, as below, is also very helpful to ADHD children since it addresses three of their problem areas: careful listening, transitions, and remembering. If you repeat the sequence, ask the children if anyone remembers what came next. Quickly changing movements forces children to pay constant attention. Vary the timing of your instructions so that they happen unexpectedly; changes or transitions that are more of a surprise are ultimately more fun.

Reactions

Except as noted

252 Dart-Slither

Begin by sitting on the floor. Tell the children: *Dart, melt, waddle, hop, caterpillar roll, wrap, pop, sneak, jump, smile, slither.*

Repeat this combination several times. Pay attention to when children begin to remember and anticipate the next movement. Then mix up the order!

253 Balance-Explode

Begin by sitting on the floor. Say: *Balance, slide, hop, shrink, cat leap, grow, bounce, kick, hover, penguin, explode.*

Try repeating words such as "balance" and "bounce" to see if the children can vary the movement.

254 Sit-Jump

Begin in a standing position. Say: *Sit, walk, spin, march, wiggle, gorilla walk, twist, smile, horse gallop, shake, freeze, jump.*

Reverse the order of the movements.

255 Float-Drip

Begin by kneeling. Say: *Float, giraffe* chassé, *vibrate, shuffle, grip, jellyfish, drip, pause, leap, pull.*

Try alternating just two words to see how fast the children can respond, such as, "Float, vibrate, float, vibrate." Vary the timing so they are always caught off guard.

Reactions

256 Whirl-Vibrate

Begin in a standing position with some space between the children. Tell them: *Whirl, dangle, relax, crumple, birdstand, anchor, frog jump, swing, jerk.*

Ask the children to use one body part at a time to do these movements; for example, "Can just your hand dangle?"

257 Press-Pop

With the class standing, say: *Compress (or press), tiptoe, shoot, seal walk, spread, splatter, cow run, sneak, pop.*

Allow the children to make sounds.

258 Stamp-Swing

With the children standing, tell them: *Stamp, flick, mule kick, collapse, swish, bunny jump, squeeze, freeze, swing.*

Try with a partner. Try mirroring the movements.

259 Stop and Go

Have the children move in some way; for example, they could pantomime a sports movement, do a creative movement such as moving like the wind, or perform a movement of their own choice. When you say, "Stop!" they freeze. When you say, "Go!" they continue. Change movements after a few repetitions.

260 Combination: Stop and Go and Touch the Floor

Have the children move around however they want. Then call out, "Stop!" and then a number such as "Three." This means that the children must stop moving and freeze with that number of body parts touching the floor. Make it challenging by having them use completely different body parts than they did in the previous turn.

Talk about what the word "isolation" means; if your students are not ready to understand, just tell them to move one body part at a time.

✱ Isolation of Body Parts ✱

261 Body Parts

Have the children stand. Allow time for them to explore each part. Tell them: *See and count how many ways you can move your arm, move your eyebrows, just one eyebrow, move your knee, move your nose, move your forehead, move your thumbs, move your hip, move your wrist, move your shoulder, move your ankle,* etc.

262 Body Part to Body Part

Ask the children to stand. Say: *Touch your toe to your knee, touch your elbow to your knee, your finger to your back, a wrist to an elbow, a shoulder to a knee, your ribs to your thigh,* etc.

263 Slow Motion

This exercise can begin in any position. Tell the children: *Slowly lift one arm. As slowly as you can, lift the other arm. Lift one leg as slowly as you can. Put it down. Slowly lift the other leg. Move through space as slowly as you can.*

Transitions in slow motion from sitting to standing and from standing to sitting are a great challenge.

✱ General Reactions ✱

264 Follow the Leader (Shadow) (whole group)

Make one child the leader and have the class follow his or her movements. This can be done in small or large groups. When the direction the group is facing changes, the person in front can become the leader.

Reactions: General Reactions

265 Mirror Image *pairs*

Have partners face one another and try to mirror every movement, even facial expressions. Try slow motion at first.

266 Side by Side *pairs*

Have partners move in unison while standing side by side. Have them see how close they can get to moving exactly alike.

404 Deskside Activities for Energetic Kids ...

Sports and Gymnastics

Sometimes pantomiming even one part of a sports movement or just imagining the toss of a basketball or baseball can bring a sense of liveliness and fun into the classroom. Learning the isolated movements of sports skills and then putting them all together is a process called "progressions"; it will help some students understand the various parts of skills and will help others improve their technique. All of the units in this chapter are structured so that the activities build on each other; therefore, I have only inserted the progression icon when a game builds on a skill from a previous unit or chapter. Although the skills are described technically and visual images for their proper execution are given, feel free to use your own developmentally appropriate language for your students. Prior to practicing the skills that use balls or rackets, the specific ball or racket called for could be passed around the classroom so the children can hold it while closing their eyes, feeling its size, and gripping it so they can commit these sensations to muscle memory. (This is merely an option, so I have not included the props icon in such activities.) This type of practice completely eliminates the competitive aspect of any sport. Even if the approach is not a highly technical one, there are no winners, losers, or stars, so it can always be fun and will make the children feel as if they have had a mini recess.

The units on body positions begin with some basic poses that evolve into more difficult ones. The use of the command style can actually be great fun for the children while they are in the process of learning the positions and their names. Call out the positions and have the children get into them as quickly as possible. If you are already using the criss-cross command for a seated position, you will be able to vary it with many of the other seated positions in this section.

The standing (gymnastics) positions actually take up less space than some of the locomotion assignments in other parts of the book. Review the rules for the children doing only what they are supposed to be doing (sometimes it is helpful to ask the ADD and ADHD children what they are supposed to be doing and have them verbally answer in order to prevent them from getting carried away in the excitement of a sports movement). Then also remind them to stay clear of one another and designate the space in which their movement should be done. Sometimes stating the number of repetitions they are to do is helpful. You will find that most of the gymnastics positions are very contained and can be practiced deskside. The sections on supports and holds are wonderful for developing core and overall body strength. Even if the children can only hold for a couple of seconds, they can better their time on their next attempt.

The first activity, overarm throwing, introduces a basic skill that is fundamental for many sports besides just baseball.

Baseball

Except as noted

267 Throwing

The overarm throw is a good movement for children to practice because it aids in the development of tracking awareness, kinesthetic awareness, and spatial awareness. Review forward arm circles (#4). Have the children watch where the throwing hand is when they release the ball. Tell the precontrol children that they need to release at eye level in order for the ball to go straight. Say: *Let go when your arm is by your eyes.*

Then have them practice with the other arm.

The following variation is wonderful for ADD and ADHD children who avoid crossing the midline of the body as well as bilateral and cross-lateral coordination altogether: Once the overarm throw has been mastered with the children aiming straight ahead, they can practice throwing across the body by aiming at the corners of the room. This is a good skill to be practiced in a confined space; doing so will keep them from turning their torsos to avoid crossing. After the children have practiced throwing to the corners, they can try a 45-degree angle. Place targets on the board or wall to help them aim.

Baseball

268 Pitch

Place a marker in front of the students that would indicate a home base. Simplify the instructions for the younger children. Tell them: *Start with both feet together, legs bent. Throw as you step forward.*

For older students, you can say: *Lean forward, pantomime agreeing to the catcher's signal, do an overarm throw, and lunge* [#319]. *Bend the front leg, shifting your weight forward toward the plate.*

269 Outfield

Have the children practice reaching up to catch a high fly ball and then quickly throwing it home. Then have them practice reaching down low to get a grounder and throwing it to first base.

270 Holding the Bat

Just having children practice holding an imaginary bat can be very helpful. Have them stand with legs slightly apart, facing sideways with the dominant hand in back (or with the nondominant side toward the pitcher). Remember that children may have different levels of fine and gross motor control on the two different sides. Let the children choose which side they want to power the bat with. Grip the imaginary bat, placing the dominant (or back) hand above the nondominant (or front) hand, leaving a small space between the bottom hand and the end of the bat.

271 Swing the Bat

Have the children stand with legs bent and slightly apart. Tell them: *Gripping the bat and keeping it at chest height, reach with it as far to the back as you can. Don't let your upper torso twist around to follow the bat as you place it behind you. When you swing the bat, keep it level or parallel to the ground as you move it forward at chest height. As the bat swings in front of you, shift your weight to your front leg.*

98 ... 404 Deskside Activities for Energetic Kids

272 Swing, Twist 👧 🪜

Say: *As you swing the bat, shift your weight forward onto your front foot (try this a few times). At the same time, also twist or rotate your hips forward. Your leg position will turn into a slight lunge* [#319].

273 Follow Through 👧 🪜

Have the children practice a few swings, adding not only a twist of the hips and shoulders but also of the wrists. Practice just the swing and wrist extension a few times. Then put it all together: *Swing, shifting your weight onto your front foot, rotate your torso, follow through with your shoulders and wrists. Now try the other side.*

Note: If you as a teacher are not familiar with the nuances of a particular skill, there will always be an eager volunteer in the class who can demonstrate and enjoy a moment of glory.

Underarm Swing

Except as noted

274 Bowling

The underarm swing can first be learned as a bowling technique with knees bent. Tell the children to start with an arm behind them, reach their fingers to the floor as their arms come forward, and let go when their arm is low to the front.

275 Underarm Swing

Next have the class try a standing underarm swing, releasing the imaginary ball at waist level. Tell the children to start with their arms at waist level behind them, draw a curve in space alongside their body, and when their arms get back up to waist level in front to let go. Have them say, "Swing, let go!" or, "Curve, let go!" Practice on the other side for ambidexterity.

276 Underarm Swing, Lunge

Once the standing underarm swing has been accomplished, add a lunge or "step out" on the opposite leg. Say: *Lift your arm behind you, and as you swing forward you lunge. Shift your weight forward, and bend your other leg at the end of the move.*

Saying "Swing, lunge" is helpful. Then change sides. The weight transfer happens with the path of the swing and should be a natural progression. You may see many children doing this movement naturally when they throw.

277 Step, Underarm Swing, Lunge

The children will step forward on the their throwing side and then lunge forward on the opposite leg as they swing their arm to release the ball. Have them say, "Step, swing, lunge" as they practice. Then change sides.

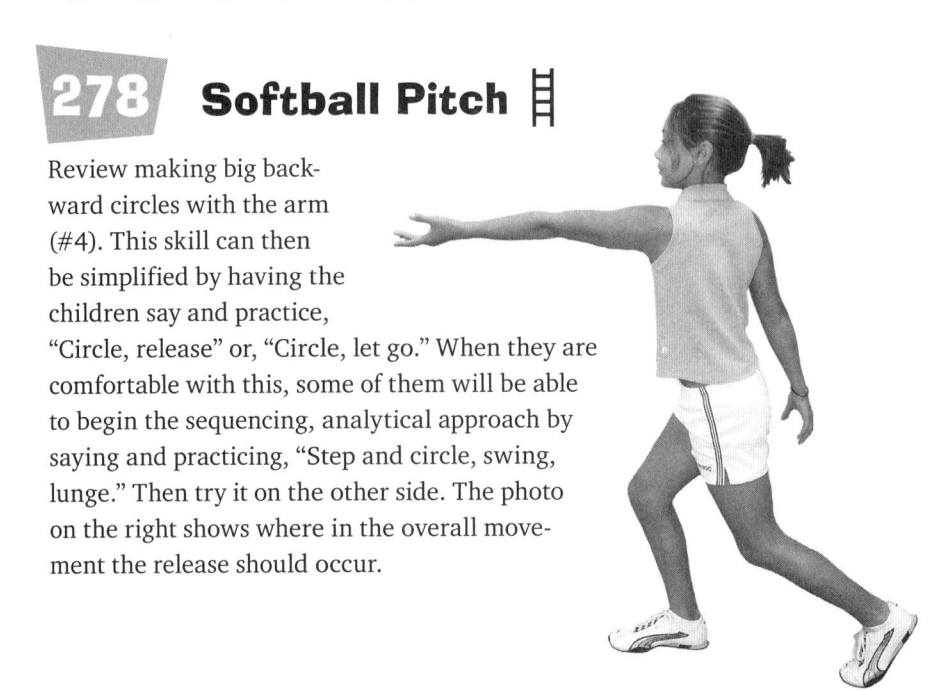

278 Softball Pitch

Review making big backward circles with the arm (#4). This skill can then be simplified by having the children say and practice, "Circle, release" or, "Circle, let go." When they are comfortable with this, some of them will be able to begin the sequencing, analytical approach by saying and practicing, "Step and circle, swing, lunge." Then try it on the other side. The photo on the right shows where in the overall movement the release should occur.

100 ... 404 Deskside Activities for Energetic Kids

Basketball

Except as noted

279 Hold, Bend, Shoot

Props (optional): Foam blocks or balls

Tell the children: *Stand with feet slightly apart. Keep your elbows close to the body. Place your hands on your imaginary basketball with your fingers spread wide apart. Try to hold the ball with your fingers and not with your palms. Bend your knees and your arms, bring the basketball to your chest, and then push the ball upward from your chest toward the basket as you straighten your legs.*

Have the children practice first without any props. Then, if you have any foam blocks, let one group at a time use the blocks to practice their aim as they throw toward an imaginary basket.

280 Jump and Shoot

Have the children stand and bend their knees and arms, bringing the imaginary basketball to their chests. Tell them to jump and throw at the same time. They can say, "Jump, shoot" or, "Bend, shoot."

Tip: Tell the older children to try to be at the top of their jump when they release the ball.

281 Jump Shot

This variation calls for a slightly more challenging way of handling the ball: shooting with one hand only. Say: *Hold the bottom of the ball with your non-dominant hand, and then push the ball into the air with your writing hand at the same time that you jump.*

Have the children try the other side. They will know immediately which hand they prefer.

282 Dribble

The children can simulate a dribble at their deskside by taking two steps to one bounce in place. Saying "Step, step, bounce; step, step, bounce" can be very helpful; however, remember to tell the children that the bounce also includes a step.

283 Bounce, Step, Bend, and Shoot

This is another possible combination. Step, land with feet together, bounce the ball, bend the knees, jump, and shoot.

Tennis, Anyone?

Except as noted

284 Ready Position

Have the children stand with legs shoulder width apart and knees bent, holding their rackets in front of them with their "good" (dominant) hand above the other hand. Say: *Do a quarter turn to the right; turn the body but keep the face looking forward (toward the net). Now turn back to the center. Do a quarter turn to the left, still looking to the front, and then turn back to center. Keep your knees bent.*

285 Handshake Grip

Help the children practice the proper grip of a tennis racket. Tell them: *You should hold the racket as if you are shaking hands with it. Keep your thumb on top. If you are a righty, hold it with your right hand. If you are a lefty, hold it with your left hand.*

102 ... 404 Deskside Activities for Energetic Kids

Tennis, Anyone?

286 Forearm Swing

Tell the class: *From the ready position [#284], make the quarter turn toward your "racket" side so that your good side is facing the back wall and your other side is facing the front wall (the net). Keep looking to the front. Use the handshake grip and practice small forward swings, keeping your forearm level (parallel) to the floor. Your thumb will stay facing the ceiling. Don't move the racket past your body or the ball will go off to the side!*

287 Backhand Swing

Have the children start in the ready position (#284). Tell them: *Do a quarter turn to the other side—toward the hand that is not holding the racket. Practice backhand strokes, keeping the arm parallel to the floor, the thumb facing the ceiling, and the top of the hand moving toward the front of the room (the net).*

288 Lob

Tell the children they can use an overarm stroke to hit high balls. Say: *Pretend a very high ball is coming toward you. Holding the racket in your dominant hand, lift it above your head, and then bend your arm so the racket touches your back. Now straighten your arm, and from up high hit the ball downward and over the net.*

289 Serve

Tell the children: *Take the racket overhead and then lower it behind you as if scratching your back. Toss the ball up with the opposite arm, and hit the ball as the racket comes up and over your head.*

Now return the serve. Say: *Hold the racket above and behind your head, and hit the ball back to your opponent.*

Golf

Except as noted

290 The Swing

Have the children stand up and grip an imaginary golf club. Tell them: *Place your hands above one another on the club, with the hand of your stronger or favorite arm on top. Keeping your eyes on the ball, lift your arms up and back behind your shoulder, and then lower them down to strike the golf ball in front of you.*

291 Weight Shift

Have *the children stand sideways, facing toward their dominant sides (their non-dominant sides should be toward the front).* Say: *Start with both knees slightly bent, lift your club upward and backward, and shift your weight to the back foot at the top of the back swing. As you swing, shift your weight forward. Always keep your eyes on the golf ball.*

292 Full Swing

Now say: *Start with your arms straight down in front of you as if your club is touching the ball. Lift your straight arms up and back, bending your knees and shifting your weight to your back foot. Shift your weight forward as you begin to swing. Follow through by wrapping your arms across your chest. Always keep your eyes on the ball.*

104 ... 404 Deskside Activities for Energetic Kids

Football

Except as noted

293 Pass

Have the children stand up and put an imaginary football in their hands. Tell them to put their fingertips right across the laces. Say: *Lean back on your favorite leg and lift your favorite arm up straight and behind your head. Pass the football while you lean forward. Shift your weight to your front foot.*

294 Punt

Have the children stand up and imagine holding a football in both hands. Tell them: *Hold your arms out straight in front of you and drop the ball. Keep pointing your toes, and kick the ball with your shoelaces (or the top of the foot) just before it reaches the ground.*

295 Catching the Ball

Ask the children to stand up and imagine a football being thrown to them. Say: *Catch the football with bent arms, pulling it in to your ribs.*

Variation: Have the children pretend they're catching the imaginary ball near a shoulder, a hip, down low, etc.

296 Jump and Catch

Ask the children to stand up and imagine a very high pass coming at them. Say: *Jump, reaching up high to catch the ball.*

297 Move to It

Ask the children to stand up and imagine a very wide pass (one that is far out to the side) coming toward them. Tell them: *Make a move to reach out, catch the ball, and bring it in to your body.*

298 Jump, Catch, Look, and Pass

Have the children stand up and imagine a high pass coming toward them. Say: *Jump and reach up high to catch the ball, run in place, lifting your knees up and down as fast as you can. Stop, then look for an opening, find it, and pass the ball to the player beside you.*

299 Pass Behind

Tell students, "While running in place, see the ball in the air coming toward you. Before the ball arrives, take a quick look behind you for another player (so that you know where you are going to throw the ball). Catch the ball, turn, and pass it to the player behind you."

300 Football Drills

Feel free to take these one session a time depending on how long you have the children run and their physical condition. Tell them: *Catch the ball and run in place, changing your feet quickly but not moving through space. Look around you while you're running to make sure no one is about to tackle you.*

Next: *Now run in place with high knees.*

Next: *Run in place with legs far apart in a wide stance.*

Next: *Run in place while kicking your heels up behind you.*

Next: *Run with the fastest feet that you can.*
Next: *Run, using your arms to help you. Pull your elbows back as you run.*

Bicycling

Except as noted

301 Upside-Down Bicycles

Have the children sit or lie down on the floor. They can lean back on their elbows or lie all the way down. Tell them: *Lift your legs up and draw circles with them as if you are riding a bike. It's uphill—push and go slow. Now it's downhill—pedal fast!*

Swimming

Except as noted

302 Crawl

Have the children stand up and lean their torsos forward. Say: *Reach one arm at a time behind your back, above you, and then down in front of you and past your torso. Breathe every three strokes by turning your head to the side.*

This can be complicated to learn in the water, so count for your students as they learn the rhythm out of the water. Count the strokes as "1, 2, 3, breathe right; 1, 2, 3, breathe left."

404 Deskside Activities for Energetic Kids ... 107

Swimming

303 Back Stroke

Have the students stand up to review backward arm circles (#4). Tell them: *Keeping your arms straight and keeping the rest of your body completely still, do backward arm circles. Then do alternating backward arm circles without moving your torso.*

Note: This is a very good exercise for shoulder flexibility.

304 Side Stroke

Have the children stand with palms facing one another in front of the ribcage area. Instruct them: *Make a figure-8 pattern with your arms while you float on the side of your body. Your top arm makes the top loop of the eight. It reaches up diagonally and pulls over the top of the shoulder while the bottom arm pushes away; then they both bend in again to loop palms past one another in front of the body.*

305 Breaststroke

Have the children stand up very straight. Say: *Lift your arms straight overhead with the backs of your hands together. Make the shape of huge bird wings by pushing your arms downward at the side of your body. Then bring the palms together up the centerline of your body. Your arms push on the way down and shoot through on the way up.*

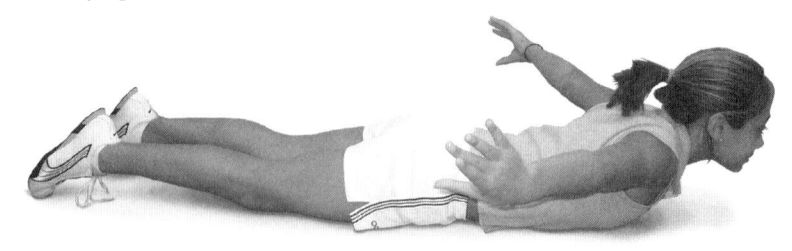

306 Butterfly Stroke

Have the children stand up and review the breaststroke (#305). Then tell them they are going to reverse the pattern. Say: *Starting with arms low at your sides,*

108 ... 404 Deskside Activities for Energetic Kids

reach them back as far as you can, and then move them up overhead and downward through the centerline of the body.

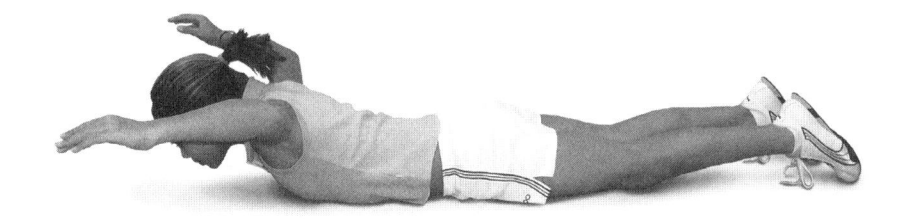

Sitting Positions

Except as noted

307 Criss-Cross, Applesauce

Tell the children: *Sit, bend your knees, and cross your legs at your ankles. Keep your back very straight. Stay tall in front, too. Try to sit up so tall that you take all the wrinkles out of your shirts!*

308 Tuck

Have the class sit down on the floor. Say: *Keep both knees together and bend them up towards your chest. Are your big toes together? Are your heels together? Are your feet pointed? Are your thighs touching your ribs? You can grab on to your knees or shins with your hands to get a tighter tuck.*

It is fun for the younger children to say the names of these positions as they learn them. Have the class try to do a tuck with a rounded back and then a tuck with a straight back.

309 Open Pike, Closed Pike

Have the students start by sitting down on the floor next to their desks. Tell them: *Sit with your legs together and extended straight out in front of you. Lift your arms straight above your head. Squeeze the muscles above your knees. Keep your back straight. This is open pike. Let's all say it so that we remember.*

Next: *Now, from open pike, reach your torso and arms to your legs, closing the angle of the pike. Try to touch your ribs to your thighs, your nose to your knees, your forehead to your shins, your fingers to your toes. This is closed pike!*

Repeat the positions a few times, saying, "Open pike, closed pike."

To do a stretching pike, have the students sit in open pike with the soles of their feet flat against a wall. Say: *Clasp your hands on top of your head, and round your back over, taking your head as low as you can. Lead downward with the top of your head. Keep both hips on the floor as you round over to the right and then to the left. Is one side of your back or one leg tighter than the other? Stretch the tighter areas twice.*

To stretch the pike even more, sit in open pike with feet flat against the wall. Tell the children: *Keep your back straight this time, and lean forward at a diagonal to create a good stretch for your back and the backs of the legs. You can reach your arms out to the side or keep them down by your sides. Try to close your pike flat.*

Sitting Positions

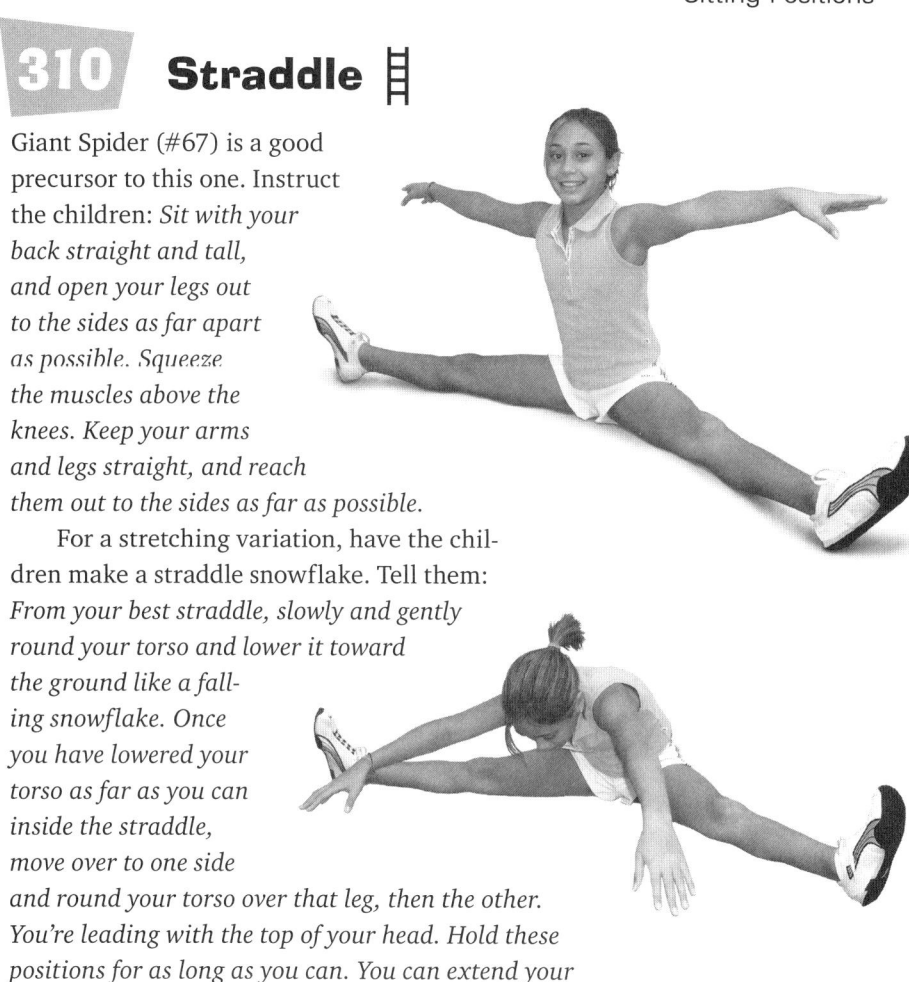

310 Straddle

Giant Spider (#67) is a good precursor to this one. Instruct the children: *Sit with your back straight and tall, and open your legs out to the sides as far apart as possible. Squeeze the muscles above the knees. Keep your arms and legs straight, and reach them out to the sides as far as possible.*

For a stretching variation, have the children make a straddle snowflake. Tell them: *From your best straddle, slowly and gently round your torso and lower it toward the ground like a falling snowflake. Once you have lowered your torso as far as you can inside the straddle, move over to one side and round your torso over that leg, then the other. You're leading with the top of your head. Hold these positions for as long as you can. You can extend your snowflake arms forward. Your snowflake should be falling closer and closer to the ground.*

Then: *To make a pancake, sit in straddle with a flat back. Keeping your back straight, not rounded, try to lower your torso to the floor between your legs, flattening your straddle like a pancake.*

404 Deskside Activities for Energetic Kids ... 111

Sitting Positions

311 Three Bears' Rocking Chairs

Here's a fun way to practice a combination of tuck (#308), pike (#309), and straddle (#310). By inverting these three positions, the children practice coordination, improve strength, and get a great stretch for the backs and legs. Tell them they are going to make the three bears' rocking chairs.

Have the children start by holding on to their knees in tuck. Have them rock backward onto their rounded backs while holding their tucks, and then roll back up to sitting while still in tuck; this is Baby Bear's rocking chair.

Next, have them get into open pike. They rock backward onto their rounded backs while maintaining their pikes, bringing their legs up into the air and overhead, trying to touch their toes to the floor behind their heads. Still in pike, they return to sitting. Talk about how this is a bigger rocking chair, Mama Bear's rocking chair. Do several repetitions.

Finally, have them get into a straddle position. Maintaining the position, they roll onto their rounded backs, lift their hips up off the floor, and try to touch their toes to the floor behind their heads in an inverted closed straddle. They roll back into sitting, still in straddle. Name the movement Papa Bear's rocking chair.

312 Stag (Side, Front, and Back)

Have the children sit in straddle (#310). Tell them the meaning of the word "stag" as it relates to deer and how they jump. Have them bend one leg inward, then straighten it and bend the other leg. Have them hold their arms out to the side. This is side stag.

For a front stag, have the children start in side stag but shift their weight and turn their torso to face the bent leg. They will need to put some weight on their hands on either side of

112 ... 404 Deskside Activities for Energetic Kids

Sitting Positions

their hips. The back leg stays extended, and the children should attempt to square their hips and shoulders to the front (the bent leg).

For a back stag, have them straighten the front leg and bend the back leg, keeping some weight on the hands and with the hips and shoulders facing the front (straight) leg.

313 *Passé* (pronounced pah-SAY)

Have the children sit in pike (#309). Then they bend one leg and touch their big toe to the opposite knee to make the shape of a triangle. Tell them to keep their ankles and feet extended or pointed.

314 V-Sit

Have the children begin by sitting in tuck (#308). Tell them: *Lean back, placing your elbows on the floor behind your hips for extra support. Keep your back straight and your chest high. Straighten both legs at a diagonal. (Hips and legs are about 90 degrees to one another; legs are about 45 degrees to the floor.) Keep your knees straight and your feet pointed. Look up and keep the chest lifted to help with balance.*

When that becomes easy, have the children lift their legs to V-sit using only their fingers on the floor for support. Keep reminding them to keep their chests high and their backs straight—this will greatly help to develop the strength for good posture and healthier backs.

404 Deskside Activities for Energetic Kids ... 113

Do an "airplane" V-sit next. Have the children go into V-sit. Then tell them: *Lift your arms out to the side. Keep your chest high.*

Without their hands on the floor, they may need to drop their legs a little lower in order to keep from rounding through the back. This works balance and core strength.

Finally, when the children can hold their arms out to the side they will be ready to do the classic V-sit. They will lift their arms to the oblique position (#341), upward and on the diagonal in a straight line with their torsos, elbows near their ears. Tell them to stay long and lifted in front and in back. Hold. Count the seconds!

Standing Positions

Except as noted

315 Straight Body

Instruct the children: *Stand up as tall as you can with feet together and straight arms stretched up to the sky.*

Note: This is a starting position for many moves in this and the next chapter.

316 Squat

A squat is a tuck (#308) that is supported by the hands as well as the feet. Say: *Start in straight body [#315]; then bend your knees until your hands touch the floor and your chest is on your thighs.*

114 ... 404 Deskside Activities for Energetic Kids

Standing Positions

317 Straddle Stand

Tell the children: *Stand up in straight body [#315], but now take your legs at least shoulder width apart and stretch your arms straight out to the sides.*

Next have the children try a piked straddle stand. Say: *Start in a straddle stand. Keeping your back flat, lean forward until your back is in a tabletop position parallel with the floor. Your arms are out to the sides.*

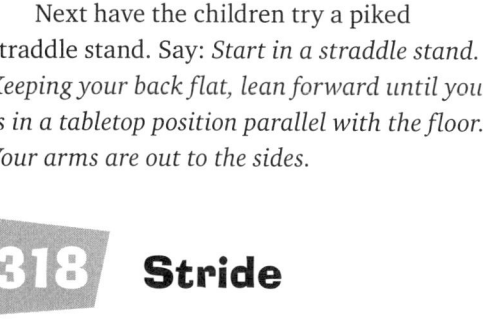

318 Stride

Instruct the children: *Stand up to begin in straight body [#315], and now take the largest step forward that you can. Keep both legs straight. Lower your arms out to the sides.*

319 Lunge (Front, Side, Back)

For a front lunge, say: *Start in stride [#318], but bend the front leg. Bring your arms up overhead. Shift your weight forward over your front foot.*

For a side lunge, tell the students: *Start in a straddle stand [#317]. Make sure your knees and toes are pointing outward. Keeping your arms out to the sides, bend one leg. Now return to straight body [#315] and then bend the other leg to lunge to the other side. Keep your knees to the sides too; don't let them drop inward.*

This exercise is good for laterality and directionality. Identify right lunge and left lunge. Review this one often.

For a back lunge, tell the children: *Start in stride [#318] but bend the back leg.*

The arms can be overhead or to the sides.

Put the combination together and have the children say, "Front lunge, side lunge, back lunge" as they execute the skills. Then have them switch sides.

404 Deskside Activities for Energetic Kids ... 115

Standing Positions

320 Standing Tuck to Standing Pike

Have the children begin in a squat (#316). Say: *Slowly straighten your legs, trying to keep your chest on your thighs until you are in a closed standing pike [#309]. Now try it by clasping your hands behind your ankles the entire time.*

Note: This stretch is great for flexibility, and because it is done in an inverted position it has the ability to wake up the students.

321 Thread the Needle

Have the children stand up and assume a standing pike (#320). Tell them: *Lift one foot and step through your arms (threading the needle) to a low stride position [#318]. Hold. Then switch legs.*

322 Hollow Body (Banana)/Arch

Have the children stand up in straight body (#315). Say: *Make a banana shape by rounding your back. Lift your arms up over your head, leaning forward slightly, and clasp your hands to make the stem.*

Now have the children try the arch. Tell them: *From the straight body [#315], look up and lift your sternum (breastbone) and your face up to the sun. Lift your ribcage up, too. Arms remain overhead. Gently arch your upper back. Do not arch your lower back. Keep your chest lifted to the sky but keep your abdominal muscles tight.*

This position is arched backward while the banana position is curved inward/forward. In the arch position only the upper body is arched; in the banana shape, the entire back is curved.

Take some time to discuss the difference between a curved (or rounded) back and an arched back. Allow children to arch their lower backs in order to feel the mistake and then correct that posture.

116 ... 404 Deskside Activities for Energetic Kids

323 Salute

Tell the students: *Make a gymnastic salute by forming a giant Y with your body. Stand up tall with your legs together. Lift your straight arms up and out on the diagonal.*

324 Pike Combination

Call out the five pike positions one after the other as a memory and speed drill. Doing this in teams is fun. Say: *Open pike* (seated with arms up), *closed pike* (seated, closing the angle of the pike by reaching the torso and arms to the legs), *standing pike* (taking a closed pike in a standing position, holding on to the feet, ankles, or legs, and trying to touch the chest to the thighs), *inverted pike* (from standing pike, bend the knees and round the back, rolling backward onto the floor with straight legs parallel over the torso), *V-sit* (rolling up into a sitting V).

Then repeat.

Note: This exercise is wonderful for the learning of levels, variations, inversion, and because it helps improve flexibility, strength, and form (which comes from repetition).

Supports

Except as noted

A support is a straight body (#315) that has at least one hand and one foot as a base of support. Ask the children to describe how the straight body shape has been changed in the following support positions (hint: the straight body shape is not vertical in these positions, and the arms are not positioned overhead).

Supports

325 Front Support

Have the children stand. Tell them that the front support position is a straight body shape (#315) in the push-up position. Say: *Put your hands and toes on the floor. Make a straight diagonal line with the your body from head to toe. Keep your arms straight. Are your abs tight?*

For younger children, explain where the abdominal muscles are located and how to tighten (contract) them. You can say: *Imagine that someone is about to accidentally bump into your stomach with their elbow. You see the elbow coming; what do you do?*

Tip: If this position is too challenging for some children, have them start with half supports, resting on knees and hands.

326 Back Support

Have the children start in a sitting pike position (#309) with their arms at their sides and their hands on the floor. Tell them: *Make sure your fingers are facing forward. Now push your body into the air to make a straight body on the diagonal with your face and tummy facing the ceiling. Squeeze all your muscles tight.*

Note: If this is too challenging for some students, have them work in crab or "table" position (#91 and #92) and do push-ups in that position to get stronger.

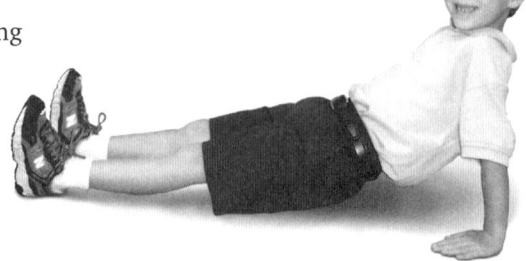

327 Side Support

Have the children begin by sitting on the floor with their legs out to one side and their hands on the floor on the other side. Tell them: *With one side facing the ceiling and the other side facing the floor, push*

118 ... 404 Deskside Activities for Energetic Kids

Supports

your body up into a straight body shape [#315], balancing on one hand and the sides of your feet. Your body will make a diagonal line and your arms will make a vertical line from hand to hand.

328 Side Support in *Passé*

Tell the children: *Get into side support [#327] and bend your top leg into a passé [#313]. Keep the triangle open. See how long you can balance. Try the other side.*

329 Side Support in Straddle (Side Star)

Say: *Get into side support [#327], and then lift your top leg to a straddle [#310]. Keep the top leg slightly turned out so that your knee faces the ceiling. See how long you can balance. Try the other side.*

330 Compass Walk

Tell the students: *Get into a side support [#327] and walk around your arm, tracing a circle with your feet like a compass. Switch hands and go the other way.*

331 Support Combination

Have the students slowly change positions. Go from front support (#325) to side support (#327), then to back support (#326) and to side support on the other side. Then start all over again on the other side.

A hold is a position that is supported completely by the hands. A fun variation is to count as high as possible during the hold. Count by 1s, 2s, 5s, etc. Even if the children at first cannot lift their bodies all the way off the floor, they can practice doing the holds until they can.

Holds

Except as noted

332 Pretzel Hold

Instruct the children: *Get into criss-cross [#307] and put your hands on the floor at your sides. Straighten your arms to push your body up off the floor.*

333 Tuck Hold

Have the children sit in tuck (#308). Then say: *Place your hands on the floor at your sides. Push down with your hands until you straighten your arms and lift your body up off the floor.*

334 Straddle Hold

Have the children sit in straddle (#310). Then say, "Place your hands inside the straddle and push down on the floor until your arms straighten, lifting your legs and hips up off the floor. Keep your chin and chest up." This is easiest when performed with legs straight and slightly turned out and with the heels placed on the inside of the straddle.

120 ... 404 Deskside Activities for Energetic Kids

Holds

335 Half L (Wolf Hold)

Have the children begin in pike (#309). Tell them: *Bend one leg into a tuck position [#308]. Put your hands on the floor at your sides. Lift yourself up off the floor by pushing down on your hands and straightening your arms.*

336 L Hold

Have the children sit in pike (#309). Say: *Place your arms at your sides and push on the floor until your arms straighten, lifting your hips and legs above the floor to form an L.*

337 V Hold

Have the children begin in a V-sit (#314). Tell them: *With your arms at your sides and your hands on the floor, push on the floor and straighten your arms until your hips lift up off the floor.*

Rhythm, Math, and Science

The total kinesthetic awareness (including awareness of extremities and facial expression) that is required in dance is the last part of physical awareness to develop in children. Therefore, I have devoted an entire section of this chapter to arm positions. Arm positions can be practiced while sitting, standing, kneeling, or lunging, or in combination with the balances described in the following section. Have the children also practice them in straddle (#310), opening the straddle a bit before going on to the next position.

The balance section can have a very calming effect on the class. Doing balance exercises is a great way to get a class to focus and concentrate. All of the balance exercises can be practiced repeatedly. Have the students remember how long they held a balance and then later try to beat their personal best. This is one of the best types of exercise for ADHD children because it requires development of control and the ability to hold still. Balances also require a tremendous amount of concentrated effort and focus. Turns, another section of the chapter, demand even more concentration, for there is balance in every turn.

Because turns incorporate balance, a good movement-education progression would be to go directly from balances to turns. Introduce the concept of visually focusing or "spotting" a turn. Do this by having the students focus their eyes on something in the direction toward which they are turning. Explain to them that their bodies will go to where they are looking or spotting. The only way to get dizzy is if they spin around without focusing on something. If they get dizzy there are two techniques to take the "dizzies" away: (1) Hold your pointer finger out in front of you with your arm straight, and focus on that finger as you pull it in to touch your nose; (2) Do tiny fast jumps up and down in place until you are no longer dizzy. The turns described here are single turns, so dizziness should not be much of a problem.

There is nothing like jumps to wake up a classroom of sleepy or tired children. Use the technique of spotting learned in the section on turns. Have the children pick out focal spots at eye level on the walls for quarter, half, and full-turn jumps. All jumps begin standing. The jumps go from symmetrical to asymmetrical in complexity.

The section on rhythm begins by simply having the children keep a steady beat. Just as in learning to count in even and odd numbers, the children will practice moving on even and odd beats. One of the goals of this section is to make them aware of the rhythms in their daily lives, such as the rhythms of their names. The sections on dance and rhythm are in the same chapter not only for the obvious reason that many dance movements are rhythmical. Jumping in half and quarter turns and moving on the half notes or in between the beats are good, concrete introductions to fractions. When the children are ready, you, the teacher, can combine assignments from these two sections and, for example, have the children do tuck jumps on the odd beats of a measure (counts 1 and 3).

Math and science are the most abstract concepts to learn and sometimes can be the most stressful subjects for children. Add some concrete, active fun to the learning of addition, subtraction, multiplication, and division just when the students least expect it and yet need it the most. Adding and subtracting people to groups are very concrete activities, as are making human sets and dividing groups of people.

Arm Positions Except as noted

338 Crown

This can be done sitting or standing. Tell the children: *Rounding your arms slightly, lift them up above your head, making a huge crown. Touch your fingers together (this is referred to as "high fifth" in ballet). Keep your shoulders down. Now completely straighten the arms for a giant king's crown.*

339 Beach Ball

With the children standing, have them place their fingertips on their belly buttons. Then they extend their arms out as far as they can while still keeping arms rounded and tips of fingers close together. Say: *Pretend that you are holding a giant beach ball in front of your tummy. Keep your chest up. Press your shoulders down.*

This is referred to as "middle fifth" in ballet.

Arm Positions

340 Low Round

Have the children stand up. Tell them: *Make your little fingers touch your thighs as you round your arms.*

Have the children round their arms, but only very slightly. In ballet, this position is called "low fifth."

Try a combination of low fifth, middle fifth, high fifth (or "low round, beach ball, crown") as the arms lift up. Then open the arms to the side and lower them down to start again.

341 Oblique

Ask the children to stand. Instruct them: *Do salute arms [#323], but take them further back behind your head to make a high backward and upward diagonal with your arms. Keep your shoulders down.*

Talk about what "oblique" means in math.

342 Opposition

Have the children stand up. Say: *Stand in stride [#318] with your right leg in front. Reach your left arm straight forward and the right arm straight out to the side.* This is opposition. The arm and leg sticking out in front are always from opposite sides (left leg and right arm, or right leg and left arm). Now start with your left leg in front.

Tell the children to make a corner where their arms meet their torsos. Talk about how opposite arms help with balance and how bent arms in opposition are used to run faster.

343 Side Middle (T Shape)

This can be done sitting or standing. Tell the children: *Stretch your arms out to the side, making a straight line from fingers to fingers. Keep your chest lifted and your shoulders down.*

This is also called "gymnastics second" if your palms are down or "jazz second" if your fingers are spread apart.

124 ... 404 Deskside Activities for Energetic Kids

344 Jazz First

This position can de done sitting or standing. Say: *Bend your arms, bringing your fingers in close to your ribs with the ends of your middle fingers touching. Your palms are either facing the floor or facing inward toward the ribs. Keep your lower arms and hands horizontal.*

345 English Hands

Have the children assume a squat (#316). Tell them: *Place your palms on the floor in front of you with the sides of your thumbs touching. Now try it in lunge [#319] by straightening one leg behind you.*

This is the starting position to go into a handstand on the balance beam. Tell the children that this hand placement is used in many skills on the balance beam.

Balances

Except as noted

346 Ruler/Eraser Balances

Tell the students: *Sitting at your desk, balance a ruler on its end in the palm of your hand. Count the number of seconds you can hold it there.*

Next: *Sitting at your desk, balance a small eraser on your nose.*

Next: *Standing, balance a ruler on your head.*

347 Walking Erasers

These balances, which involve walking forward, can be done in turns or as relays to avoid players bumping into one another. Have one child per aisle walk

Balances

forward while balancing a large eraser on his or her head. Then have one child per aisle walk forward while balancing an eraser on the top of each hand.

348 Tuck Stand

Have the children assume a squat (#316). Then say: *Shift your weight forward onto the balls of your feet until your heels come off the floor. Lift your arms out to the side. Keep your chest directly above your hips.*

Remind them to keep their chests up by telling them that it is a "tuck stand" and not a "duck stand"; show them the difference between a lifted and a dropped chest.

349 *Relevé* (pronounced reh-luh-VAY)

Have the children stand. Tell them: *Rise up as high as you can on the balls of your feet. Keep reaching the top of your head up toward the ceiling. Try balancing with your arms out to the side.*

Have them try any of the arm positions (#338–345) in *relevé*.

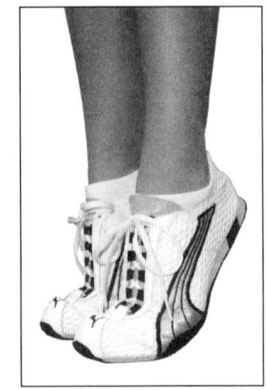

350 Elevator

Tell the children: *Start in tuck stand [#348], and slowly rise up through standing to relevé [#349], way up on your toes. Count the floors as you go. Take the elevator back down to tuck stand on the bottom floor, counting backwards as you go.*

126 ... 404 Deskside Activities for Energetic Kids

Balances

351 Knee Stand

Have the children stand on both knees to balance. Say: *Place your hips directly in line with your knees and shoulders. Now shift your weight from side to side. Next, see what piking, or bending, at the hips does to this balance.*

Use penguin arms and fish swims for fun variations.

352 Kneel

Have the children assume a knee stand (#351). Step forward onto one foot, keeping that leg bent. Lift the arms in opposition (#342; the arm of the front leg out to the side and the other arm forward). Switch sides.

353 Knee Scale

Ask the children to stand up. Tell them: *Place your hands and knees on the floor. Extend one leg straight out behind you, keeping it parallel to the floor.* (The young ones will like to say, "Knee scale, doggie tail.")

Next, say: *Now perform a knee scale by lifting one leg behind you and the opposite arm out in front of you. If you lifted your right leg, lift your left arm. If you lifted your left leg, lift your right arm. Switch sides.*

354 Free Knee Scale

Have the children begin in a knee scale (#353). Then tell them: *Lift both arms out to the sides and slightly behind your shoulders for balance. Don't let your torso come upright; keep it forward.*

404 Deskside Activities for Energetic Kids ... 127

Balances

355 Standing *Passé*

Have the students start by standing in first position (#359). Then they lift one leg into *passé* (#313), with the knee out to the side and the big toe touching the bottom corner of the supporting knee. Say: *Keep the standing leg very straight by pulling up the kneecap. Keep your hips parallel to the floor; don't let the hip of the* passé *leg rise up.*

Tell them that in terms of ballet, the French word *passé* means "pass through." Switch legs.

For a greater challenge, try *passé* in *relevé*. Tell them: *Standing in* passé, *rise up on your toes to* relevé *[#349] and see how long you can balance.*

Count, "1001, 1002," etc., or by 2s, 5s, or any multiple. Try different arm positions for balance (beach ball, crown, etc.). Switch legs.

356 Thigh Balance

Have the children stand in *passé* (#355), lifting the *passé* leg until the thigh is parallel to the floor. They then can try to balance a ruler or eraser on that thigh.

Then have the children try the same thing in *passé relevé*. Have them do this exercise on both legs.

357 *Coupé* (pronounced coo-PAY)

Tell the children that *coupé* comes from a French word that means to "cut under." Then say: *Balance on one foot and bring your big toe to the ankle of the standing leg. Rise up on your toes to* relevé *[#349]. See how long you can hold the balance.*

Switch legs.

358 Hokey Pokey Challenge

Standing in small circles, start by doing the familiar version of the Hokey Pokey:

You put your right leg in (touching right toes on the floor in front of you)
You put your right leg out (touching right toes on the floor behind you)

128 ... *404 Deskside Activities for Energetic Kids*

You put your right leg in and you shake it all about (shaking right leg)
You do the Hokey Pokey and you turn yourself around (turn around)
That's what it's all about! (clap, clap)

Do both sides as a warm up.

Then perform each side while keeping the working leg off the floor for the entire song.

Advanced Variation: Next, for a balance challenge, do the Hokey Pokey on your tiptoes (in *relevé*, #349). Then try it in *relevé* **and** with the working foot off the floor!

Dance Positions and Scales

Except as noted

All of the standing scales have slightly turned-out legs for better balance and range of motion.

359 Pizza Slice (First Position)

Teach the children to turn their legs out from their hip sockets so as not to put pressure on their knees. To do this, have them stand in straight body (#315) with arms down at their sides, extend a straight leg with a pointed foot in front of them, flex the foot, externally rotate or turn out the foot, and bring it back to touch the other heel, putting weight on it. Do the same on the other leg. The children should end up in a stance with heels together and toes apart, forming a shape that looks like an open triangle or pizza slice (ballet first position) with their natural amount of rotation.

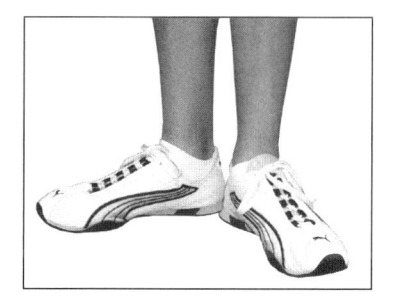

404 Deskside Activities for Energetic Kids ... 129

Dance Positions and Scales

360 First and Second Poem

Here's a fun way to teach first and second positions. Begin by standing in a straight body position (#315) with arms at sides. The class will enjoy reciting this poem:

Heels together, toes apart
> (rotate legs and open feet to first position or "pizza slice" [#359])

That's how first position starts
Point your foot to the side
> (extend a turned-out leg to the side; keep knee facing out)

Our second position is wide
> (shift weight to both feet, which are now shoulder width apart)

Our arms are low in first
> (shift weight to one foot, and bring the backs of the heels together again to return to first, with arms in first or low round, #340)

They can do a sunburst with their arms: Keeping arms curved, bring them up to crown (#338) while the foot points and extends; and then open arms to the side when the feet are in second, keeping elbows round and hands soft. Arms are lowered again to first (low round, #340) when the last line is recited.

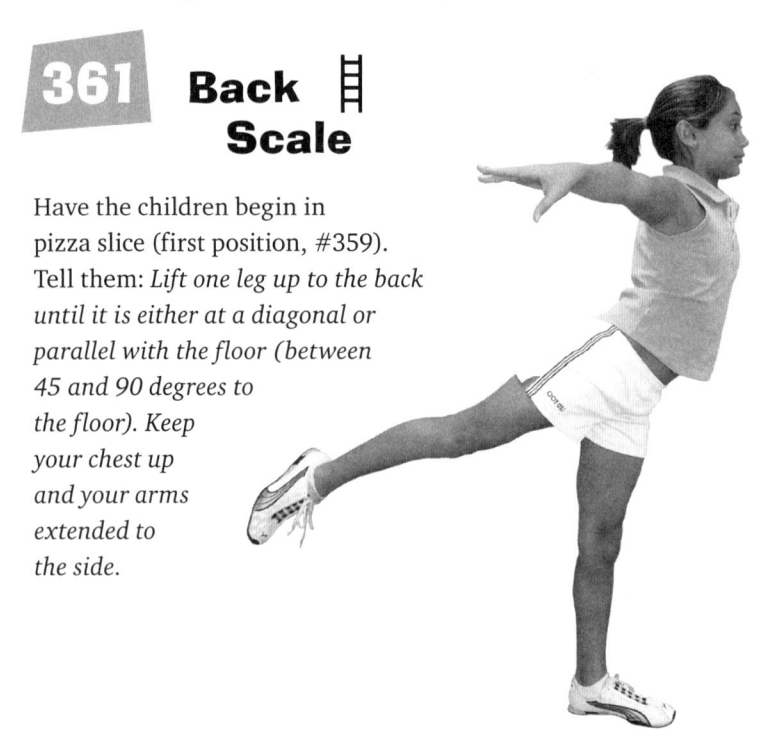

361 Back Scale

Have the children begin in pizza slice (first position, #359). Tell them: *Lift one leg up to the back until it is either at a diagonal or parallel with the floor (between 45 and 90 degrees to the floor). Keep your chest up and your arms extended to the side.*

130 ... 404 Deskside Activities for Energetic Kids

Dance Positions and Scales

362 Side Scale

Have the children stand in pizza slice (first position, #359). Say: *Lift one leg (you may want to designate right or left) up to the side as high as you can (between 45 and 90 degrees to the floor). Keep your knee facing the ceiling. Keep your shoulders and hip bones level. Reach your arms out to the side.*

363 Front Scale

Have the children stand in pizza slice (first position, #359). Say: *Lift one leg up to the front as high as you can (between 45 and 90 degrees to the floor). Keep the heel of your standing leg, belly button, and nose all in the same vertical line. Keep your standing leg straight, your back straight, your chest lifted, and your arms straight out to the side. Now try your other leg.*

364 Y-Scale

Instruct the class: *Perform a side scale [#362], but use your arm to lift your free leg. Lift your other arm up on a diagonal to create a Y shape with your body.*

365 Front/Back Attitude

Tell the class: *Do a front scale [#363], but bend the knee and lift the heel of the working leg. Keep the standing leg very straight. Switch legs.*

This is the position for cat leaps (#107) and front stag jumps (#386).

Next, say: *Do a back scale [#361], but bend the working knee, keeping it as high as possible. Keep the standing leg very straight. Switch legs.*

This is the position for back stag jumps (#386).

366 T-Scale

Have the children start in a front lunge (#319) with their arms overhead. Tell them: *Lift the back leg off the floor, making a straight line from your fingers down your spine to the toes of the leg that's lifted. You're using your body, arms, and legs to make a horizontal T that is parallel to the floor. Hold this position for as long as you can.*

Have them switch legs.

404 Deskside Activities for Energetic Kids ... 131

367 Lever (Teeter-Totter)

Tell the students: *Start in a front lunge [#319]. Make a T-scale [#366], but continue reaching downward on a diagonal until your fingers touch the floor. Remember, stay in a straight line from fingers to toes. Return to the T position and back to the lunge. Switch sides.*

Turns

Except as noted

A moderate space is needed for some turns.

368 Sit and Spin

Have the children sit with legs crossed and push with their hands on the floor to turn themselves around.

369 Tuck-Stand Turn

Have the children begin in tuck stand (#348). Tell them: *To do a half turn in tuck stand, look at the wall in front of you, then turn to look at the wall behind you. Keep your chest lifted the entire time. Try this turn with your arms out to the sides. Then try it with your arms up above your head. Lastly, try it with your arms up, then open them to stop the turn and balance.*

370 Pivot Turn

Have the class stand. Tell them: *With one leg in front of the other, get on your tiptoes in* relevé *[#349], and do a half turn toward your back leg.*

371 Elevator Up and Down

Have everyone begin in tuck stand (#348). Say: *Go up all the floors to relevé [#349], turn around (pivot turn), and go back down. Pivot around (in tuck stand) and go back up.*

372 Soutenu
(pronounced soot-NU)

Tell the students: *Standing, bend your free leg, and cross it over the standing one. Plant the ball of your foot on the floor, and turn toward your crossed leg until your legs uncross.*

Jumps

Except as noted

All of the jumps build on the first two activities, Safe Landing Position and Stretch Jump. Make sure the children know these moves well before proceeding to the more advanced jumps. A moderate space is needed for larger jumps.

373 Safe Landing Position

Before practicing a big jump, students need to learn how to land in the safe landing position, or SLP. Tell the children to lift straight arms up by their ears; keep shoulders down. The legs are parallel to one another, with feet facing straight ahead, and the knees are slightly bent. Have the children practice jumping and landing with their arms up, their backs straight and vertical, and their shoulders directly above their hips as their knees bend. Have the

Jumps

children say "Up, SLP" to help them realize that the jump and the landing are two separate parts of the movement.

374 Stretch Jump

Instruct the class: *With legs together, swing your arms overhead as you jump up straight in the air. Land in SLP [#373].*

To use the feet properly, the children should push off "heel-ball-toe" and land "toe-ball-heel." Have them say, "Jump, SLP," or, "Jump, 1, 2, 3." Have them listen to their landings to determine whether they are using all three parts of their feet.

Now you may proceed to half-turn jumps or quarter-turn jumps. The quarter-turn jumps are easier physically but are a more difficult math concept than halves.

375 Jumping Fractions
(Half-Turn Jumps)

Tell the students to stand and to pick out something on the wall directly in front of them and something on the wall directly behind them; these are their spots. Say: *Do stretch jumps [#374] with a half turn, looking to the back wall as soon as you jump up. Then jump again, looking to the front wall.*

Have them say, "Jump, look" to help them continue spotting the walls. Have them land in SLP (#373).

376 More Jumping Fractions
(Quarter-Turn Jumps)

Quarter turns are the easiest variation of turning jumps. The children should have great fun doing them. Have the children stand and pick something directly in front of them on each wall. To help teach the concept of fourths, tell the children that the room is divided into four walls or four quarters. Then let them experience this concept by jumping it. Have them say, "Up, look" each time they do a stretch jump, looking to each wall in turn and landing in SLP (#373). Once they get the idea of spotting they can count "up, 1, up, 2," etc., or in fourths as they go. Then switch directions.

134 ... 404 Deskside Activities for Energetic Kids

Jumps

377 Full-Turn Jumps

Have the students do a full turning jump, starting from straight body (#315). Remind them to visually spot something on the wall directly in front of them and to go up before they turn. Say, "Up, turn," "Jump, turn," or, "Jump, look." If children appear to be twisting on the way up and are landing off balance, they are most likely turning too soon on the way up instead of waiting until the top of the jump.

378 Tuck Jump

Have the children start in straight body (#315). Then tell them: *Put a tuck position [#308] in the air by jumping and pulling your knees up to your chest.*
 Say: *Put a tuck in the sky*
 Or
 Make your knees touch your shirt.
 To avoid leaning forward, say: *Bring your knees to your chest and not your chest to your knees.*

379 Straddle Jump

Have the children begin in straight body (#315). Then say: *Put a straddle [#310] in the air by jumping and opening your legs wide. Think, "open, close" in the air.*

Have the more advanced students turn out their legs to get more height. Tell them to keep their knees facing the sky or ceiling and not the wall or the teacher in front of them. For this jump the arms can parallel the legs in an "open, close" movement to the sides.

380 Hitch Kick

Have the children stand. Tell them: *Keeping your back straight and your legs straight, kick your legs in front of you one at a time, but as quickly as you can.*

Both legs will be off the floor at the same time for a moment. Have the children say, "Kick kick," or, "Hitch kick." The arms can move up and open in the same quick rhythm.

404 Deskside Activities for Energetic Kids ... **135**

Jumps

381 Jump Combination

Have the students do stretch jump (#374), tuck jump (#378), and straddle jump (#379). See how many sets they can do. This is a very good combination for the development of progressive thought.

382 Pike Jump

Have the children start in straight body (#315). Tell them: *Put a pike [#309] in the sky by lifting both legs straight up in front of you while you jump.*

Explain that this is the most difficult jump they have done so far. They can either try to touch their toes or keep their arms to the side for balance.

383 *Assemblé* (pronounced ah-sahm-BLAY)

Tell the class that their legs will *assemblé* (French for "assemble") in the air. Say: *Stand on one leg, and jump to land on two feet. Make your legs come together in the air right before your feet touch down.*

384 *Sissoné* (pronounced see-sahn-AY)

Tell the children that *sissonés* and *assemblés* (#383) are opposites in that *assemblé* goes from one to two feet and *sissoné* goes from two to one foot. Say: *Jump from two feet to land on one. Bend the landing leg. Take your arms out to the sides for balance.*

Have the children try both sides. For a challenge have them try landing in a scale.

385 Split Jump

Have the children jump as they split their legs in stride (#318), one in front and one in back. Tell them: *Try to make the straightest line possible in the sky.*

Because they need to start in a deep knee bend, they can also say, "Bend, pull," or, "Push, pull" as they push off the floor and pull their legs apart.

386 Front, Back, and Double Stag Jumps

Tell the students: *Do a split jump [#385], this time bending the front leg under you like a deer for a front stag jump. Try to make the lower part of your leg (calf) touch the back of your thigh.*

Next: *Now do a split jump, bending the back leg behind you for a back stag jump.*

Next: *Do a split jump, this time bending both legs to perform a double stag jump.*

387 Herds of Deer

Have the students travel around the room doing different types of stag jumps in trios of deer, and then in larger groups of deer.

Rhythm and Clapping Activities

Except as noted

388 Steady Beat

Have the whole class keep a steady beat by clapping. Then count in measures of 2s, 3s, 4s, 6s, 8s, or even 5s. Do this by emphasizing the first beat of the measure (e.g., for a beat of four: <u>1</u>, 2, 3, 4, <u>1</u>, 2, 3, 4).

389 Peter Works

Start with one fist as a drum (on a desktop or in the palm of the other hand) and then add a body part with every verse:

Peter works with one hammer, one hammer, one hammer (thumping one fist on the desk)

404 Deskside Activities for Energetic Kids ... 137

Peter works with one hammer all day long
Peter works with two hammers, two hammers, two hammers (using two fists)
Peter works with two hammers all day long
Peter works with three hammers...(using two fists and one foot stomping on the ground)
Peter works with four hammers...(using two fists and two feet)
Peter works with five hammers...(using two fists, two feet, and a head nod)

390 Echo

Play Follow the Leader in rhythm by having a student or teacher clap out a rhythm and then having the whole class repeat it. The leader then designates a new leader.

391 My Name Symphony

Talk about how everyone's name has a rhythm. Have the students practice clapping the rhythm of their first names. Count out "1, 2, ready, go" to establish a steady beat even though this will end up creating counter rhythms as the students clap the rhythm of their first names together.

Then have everyone practice the rhythm of their first and last names together. Get them to say their formal names rhythmically to a beat. Have them say their names to a beat in polyphony. Then have them clap the rhythm of their names within the same three measures.

392 Full Name Symphony

Make a symphony out of the rhythm of people's full names. Have solo recitation or clapping row by row. Then have a grand finale with the whole class together. (The teacher's name should have a solo too.)

393 Echo My Name

Combine the two symphonies by having a student stand up and clap the rhythm of his first name. Then have everyone who has that rhythm in their first name stand up and echo the rhythm. Go through the classroom student by student.

394. 1 and 3, 2 and 4

Count out a steady four-beat rhythm. Have the students move, march, or clap only on beats 1 and 3. Just stepping on these beats is enough of a project at first.
Now move or make shapes only on beats 2 and 4.

395. Off Beat

Clap on beats 1, 2, 3, and 4. Have the children move on the "and," or the space in between the beats.

396. Choose the Beats

Within an eight-beat measure, have the children choose on which beats they will move.

Math and Science

Except as noted

397. Human Links: Addition

Call out a number, such as six, and have the children link arms to show what (how many) plus what (how many) equals six. For instance, if two people link, then four others must link.

398. Human Links: Subtraction

Call out an answer such as two. The students have to show what makes two as the answer; so four link and then two link, or six link and then four link. See how many possibilities there are in the classroom.

404 Deskside Activities for Energetic Kids ... 139

Math and Science

399 Human Division

Divide groups of people. This can help even children who are not dividing yet. First, talk about dividing a cookie to share it with a friend, then two friends, etc. Then the class can be divided into two groups, three groups, etc., and then into groups of two, groups of three, etc.

400 Human Sets

The class can form groups of threes, then fours, and so on, to introduce the concept of sets. After the class has formed sets, they can then add, multiply, subtract, or divide their sets by physically moving to new locations. Give instructions according to what the class is studying at the time.

401 Human Links: Multiplication

Call out an answer such as four. As with the addition and subtraction games (#397 and #398), have the students link arms in two groups that, multiplied together, would produce that answer; for example, two linking with two, four linking with one.

402 Human Links: Division

Call out a number such as two. To answer, the students would link in groups of four and two, or six and three, etc., to show two numbers that would divide to produce that answer.

403 Planets Rotating

To show rotation *and* revolution, have the children who are the planets do forward rolls in a circle around the sun. To do a forward roll, have the children start in a straight body position (#315) and then reach down to the floor while rounding their backs. With their hands on the floor, they tuck their chins so that the backs of their heads touch the floor first, and then they roll down the rest

Math and Science

of their spines while in tuck (#308), standing up through a tuck stand (#348) to start another day!

404 Solar System

Choose one person to be the sun and others to be the planets. Have the planets revolve (walk) in a circle around the sun.

References

Abramovitz, B. A., and L. L. Birch. 2000. "Five-Year-Old Girls' Ideas about Dieting Are Predicted by Their Mothers' Dieting." *Journal of the American Dietetic Association* 100(10): 1157–63.

Berenson, G. S. (ed.). 1980. *Cardiovascular Risk Factors in Children: The Early Natural History of Atherosclerosis and Essential Hypertension.* New York: Oxford University Press.

Cleland, F. 1990. "How Many Ways Can I…? Problem Solving Through Movement." In W. J. Stinson (ed.), *Moving and Learning for the Young Child* (pp. 73–76). Reston, VA: American Alliance for Health, Physical Education, Recreation and Dance.

Dudek, S. 1974. "Creativity in Young Children: Attitude or Ability?" *Journal of Creative Behavior* 8: 282–92.

Gardner, Howard. 1983. *Frames of Mind.* New York: Basic Books.

Gardner, Howard. 1993. *Multiple Intelligences.* New York: Basic Books.

Graham, G. 1992. *Teaching Children Physical Education.* Champaign, IL: Human Kinetics.

Groves, D. 1988. "Is Childhood Obesity Related to TV Addiction?" *The Physician and Sportsmedicine* 16 (11): 117–122.

Mosston, M., and Ashworth, S. 1990. *The Spectrum of Teaching Styles: From Command to Discovery.* New York: Longman.

Nichter, M. 2000. *Fat Talk: What Girls and Their Parents Say about Dieting.* Cambridge, MA: University Press.

Ross, J. G., Pate, R. R., Lohman, T. G., and Christenson, G. M. 1987. "Changes in Body Composition of Children." *Journal of Physical Recreation and Dance* 58 (9): 74–77.

Activities with Special Requirements

Activities for Advanced Players

321	Thread the Needle	364	Y-Scale
328	Side Support in *Passé*	367	Lever (Teeter-Totter)
329	Side Support in Straddle (Side Star)	379	Straddle Jump
		381	Jump Combination
331	Support Combination	382	Pike Jump
332	Pretzel Hold	385	Split Jump
333	Tuck Hold	386	Front, Back, and Double Stag Jumps
334	Straddle Hold		
335	Half L (Wolf Hold)	387	Herds of Deer
336	L Hold	395	Off Beat
337	V Hold	403	Planets Rotating
354	Free Knee Scale	404	Solar System
355	Standing *Passé*		

Activities Requiring Physical Contact

144	Train	204	Jumping Criss-Cross Sailor
196	Flower Sit-Ups	243	Forward/Backward Shape
201	Jungle River	249	Partner Shape
202	A Sailor Went to Sea	250	Shifting Shape
203	Jumping Sailor	251	Jungle Gym

Activities Requiring Props

- 84 Row Relay
- 85 Toss and Answer
- 129 Puppet Walks
- 279 Hold, Bend, Shoot

Activities Requiring a Large Space

24	Group Rainbow	101	Baby Bear Walk
95	Duck Walk	102	Camel Walk
98	Sandpiper	104	Caterpillar Roll
100	Bear Walk	106	Gator Walk

404 Deskside Activities for Energetic Kids ... **143**

109	Cow Running	218	Looking for an Elephant
110	Horse Gallop	243	Forward/Backward Shape
111	Giraffe *Chassé*	246	Sideward Shape
116	Monkey with a Tail in the Air	250	Shifting Shape
118	Horse Kick	251	Jungle Gym
119	Mule Kick	252	Dart-Slither
120	Spider Walk	253	Balance-Explode
121	Low Walk/High Walk	254	Sit-Jump
122	Center Walk	255	Float-Drip
123	Toe-Ball-Heel Walk	256	Whirl-Vibrate
126	Weather Walk	257	Press-Pop
127	Head Walks	258	Stamp-Swing
128	Torso Walks	259	Stop and Go
130	Arm and Shoulder Walks	260	Combination: Stop and Go and Touch the Floor
131	Toddler		
132	Wearing a Cast	309	Open Pike, Closed Pike
133	Old Walk	311	Three Bears' Rocking Chairs
134	Emotional Walk	321	Thread the Needle
135	I'm Late!	330	Compass Walk
136	Mad	347	Walking Erasers
137	Look Out!	366	T-Scale
142	Wave	367	Lever (Teeter-Totter)
143	Balloon	379	Straddle Jump
144	Train	381	Jump Combination
147	Top	382	Pike Jump
155	Walk the Dog	385	Split Jump
159	Picking Apples	386	Front, Back, and Double Stag Jumps
166	Kickboxer		
196	Flower Sit-Ups	387	Herds of Deer
205	Classroom Wave	403	Planets Rotating
208	Sea Anemones	404	Solar System
214	Big Kicks on the Moon		

Activities That Require Knowledge Learned in Another Activity

30	Knee 8s	101	Baby Bear Walk
31	Toe 8s	113	Hungry Seal
38	Standing Letters	119	Mule Kick
49	Diving Arms	218	Looking for an Elephant
92	Crab Push-Ups	233	Two Hands, One Leg

234	Head, Hand, Foot	356	Thigh Balance
236	Side	357	*Coupé*
237	Twenty Bases	360	First and Second Poem
267	Throwing	361	Back Scale
272	Swing, Twist	362	Side Scale
273	Follow Through	363	Front Scale
276	Underarm Swing, Lunge	364	Y-Scale
277	Step, Underarm Swing, Lunge	365	Front/Back Attitude
278	Softball Pitch	366	T-Scale
280	Jump and Shoot	367	Lever (Teeter-Totter)
281	Jump Shot	369	Tuck-Stand Turn
283	Bounce, Step, Bend, and Shoot	370	Pivot Turn
286	Forearm Swing	371	Elevator Up and Down
287	Backhand Swing	374	Stretch Jump
291	Weight Shift	375	Jumping Fractions (Half-Turn Jumps)
292	Full Swing	376	More Jumping Fractions (Quarter-Turn Jumps)
303	Back Stroke	377	Full-Turn Jumps
310	Straddle	378	Tuck Jump
328	Side Support in *Passé*	379	Straddle Jump
329	Side Support in Straddle (Side Star)	381	Jump Combination
332	Pretzel Hold	382	Pike Jump
333	Tuck Hold	383	*Assemblé*
334	Straddle Hold	385	Split Jump
335	Half L (Wolf Hold)	386	Front, Back, and Double Stag Jumps
336	L Hold	387	Herds of Deer
337	V Hold	392	Full Name Symphony
341	Oblique	393	Echo My Name
342	Opposition	395	Off Beat
345	English Hands	396	Choose the Beats
350	Elevator	403	Planets Rotating
352	Kneel		
354	Free Knee Scale		
355	Standing *Passé*		

SmartFun Activity Books

SmartFun activity books encourage imagination, social interaction, and self-expression in children. Games are organized by the skills they develop, and simple icons indicate appropriate age levels, times of play, and group size. Most games are noncompetitive and require no special training. The series is widely used in schools, homes, and summer camps.

101 RELAXATION GAMES FOR CHILDREN: Finding a Little Peace and Quiet In Between by Allison Bartl

The perfect antidote for unfocused and fidgety young children, these games help to maintain or restore order, refocus children's attention, and break up classroom routine. Most games are short and can be used as refreshers or treats. They lower noise levels in the classroom and help to make learning fun. **Ages 6 and up.**

>> 128 pages ... 96 illus. ... Paperback $14.95 ... Spiral bound $19.95

101 PEP-UP GAMES FOR CHILDREN: Refreshing, Recharging, Refocusing by Allison Bartl

Children get re-energized with these games! Designed for groups of mixed-age kids, the games require little or no preparation or props, with easier games toward the beginning and more advanced ones toward the end. All games are designed to help children release pent-up energy by getting them moving. **Ages 6–10.**

>> 128 pages ... 86 illus. ... Paperback $14.95 ... Spiral bound $19.95

101 QUICK-THINKING GAMES + RIDDLES FOR CHILDREN by Allison Bartl

The 101 games and 65 riddles in this book will engage and delight students and bring fun into the classroom. All the games, puzzles, and riddles work with numbers and words, logic and reasoning, concentration and memory. Children use their thinking and math and verbal skills while they sing, clap, race, and read aloud. Certain games also allow kids to share their knowledge of songs, fairytales, and famous people. **Ages 6–10.**

>> 144 pages ... 95 illus. ... Paperback $14.95 ... Spiral bound $19.95

101 MOVEMENT GAMES FOR CHILDREN: Fun and Learning with Playful Movement by Huberta Wiertsema

Movement games help children develop sensory awareness and use movement for self-expression. The games are in sections including reaction games, cooperation games, and expression games, and feature old favorites such as Duck, Duck, Goose as well as new games such as Mirroring, Equal Pacing, and Moving Joints. **Ages 6 and up.**

>> 160 pages ... 49 illus. ... Paperback $14.95 ... Spiral bound $19.95

To order visit www.hunterhouse.com or call (800)-266-5592

More *SmartFun* Activity Books pg. 2

101 MUSIC GAMES FOR CHILDREN: Fun and Learning with Rhythm and Song *by Jerry Storms*

All you need to play these games are music CDs and simple instruments, many of which kids can make from common household items. Many games are good for large group settings, such as birthday parties, others are easily adapted to classroom needs. No musical knowledge is required. **Ages 4 and up.**

>> 160 pages ... 30 illus. ... Paperback $14.95 ... Spiral bound $19.95

101 MORE MUSIC GAMES FOR CHILDREN: New Fun and Learning with Rhythm and Song *by Jerry Storms*

This action-packed compendium offers musical activities that children can play while developing a love for music. Besides concentration and expression games, this book includes relaxation games, card and board games, and musical projects. **A multicultural section** includes songs and music from Mexico, Turkey, Surinam, Morocco, and the Middle East. **Ages 6 and up.**

>> 176 pages ... 78 illus. ... Paperback $14.95 ... Spiral bound $19.95

101 DANCE GAMES FOR CHILDREN: Fun and Creativity with Movement *by Paul Rooyackers*

These games encourage children to interact and express how they feel in creative ways, without words. They include meeting and greeting games, cooperation games, story dances, party dances, "musical puzzles," dances with props, and more. No dance training or athletic skills are required. **Ages 4 and up.**

>> 160 pages ... 36 illus. ... Paperback $14.95 ... Spiral bound $19.95

101 MORE DANCE GAMES FOR CHILDREN: New Fun and Creativity with Movement *by Paul Rooyackers*

Designed to help children develop spontaneity and cultural awareness, the games in this book include Animal Dances, Painting Dances, Dance Maps, and Story Dances. The **Dance Projects from Around the World** include Hula Dancing, Caribbean Carnival, Chinese Dragon Dance, and Capoeira. **Ages 4 and up.**

>> 176 pages ... 44 b/w photos. ... Paperback $14.95 ... Spiral bound $19.95

101 LANGUAGE GAMES FOR CHILDREN: Fun and Learning with Words, Stories and Poems *by Paul Rooyackers*

Language is perhaps the most important human skill, and play can make language more creative and memorable. The games in this book have been tested in classrooms around the world. They range from letter games to word play, story-writing, and poetry games, including Hidden Word and Haiku Arguments. **Ages 4 and up.**

>> 144 pages ... 27 illus. ... Paperback $14.95 ... Spiral bound $19.95

Free shipping on all personal website orders

More *SmartFun* Activity Books   pg. 3

101 DRAMA GAMES FOR CHILDREN: Fun and Learning with Acting and Make-Believe by Paul Rooyackers

Drama games are a fun, dynamic form of play that help children explore their imagination and creativity. These noncompetitive games include introduction games, sensory games, pantomime games, story games, sound games, games with masks, games with costumes, and more. **Ages 4 and up.**

>> 160 pages ... 30 illus. ... Paperback $14.95 ... Spiral bound $19.95

101 MORE DRAMA GAMES FOR CHILDREN: New Fun and Learning with Acting and Make-Believe by Paul Rooyackers

These drama games require no acting skills — just an active imagination. The selection includes morphing games, observation games, dialog games, living video games, and game projects. **A special multicultural section** includes games on Greek drama, African storytelling, Southeast Asian puppetry, Pacific Northwest transformation masks, and Latino folk theater. **Ages 6 and up.**

>> 144 pages ... 35 illus. ... Paperback $14.95 ... Spiral bound $19.95

101 IMPROV GAMES FOR CHILDREN AND ADULTS
by Bob Bedore

Improv comedy offers the next step in drama and play: creating something out of nothing, reaching people using talents you don't know you possess. With exercises for teaching improv to children, advanced improv techniques, and tips for thinking on your feet — all from an acknowledged master of improv. **Ages 5 and up.**

>> 192 pages ... 65 b/w photos ... Paperback $14.95 ... Spiral bound $19.95

YOGA GAMES FOR CHILDREN: Fun and Fitness with Postures, Movements and Breath
by Danielle Bersma and Marjoke Visscher

A playful introduction to yoga, these games help young people develop body awareness, physical strength, and flexibility. The 54 activities are variations on traditional yoga exercises, clearly illustrated. Ideal for warm-ups and relaxing time-outs. **Ages 6–12.**

>> 160 pages ... 57 illus. ... Paperback $14.95 ... Spiral bound $19.95

THE YOGA ADVENTURE FOR CHILDREN: Playing, Dancing, Moving, Breathing, Relaxing by Helen Purperhart

Offers an opportunity for the whole family to laugh, play, and have fun together. This book explains yoga stretches and postures as well as the philosophy behind yoga. The exercises are good for a child's mental and physical development, and also improve concentration and self-esteem. **Ages 4–12.**

>> 144 pages ... 75 illus. ... Paperback $14.95 ... Spiral bound $19.95

To order visit www.hunterhouse.com or call (800)-266-5592

Magical Mandala Coloring Books

Mandalas represent wholeness and life. Their designs and patterns are taken from geometry, nature, and folk art. Made up of simple elements, yet often marvelously complex, they fascinate children and adults alike. Mandalas have been found in prehistoric caves, ancient tapestries, and the art of people all over the world. These three mandala books make wonderful gifts for children and parents, and can be used anywhere — all you need is a set of colored pens, pencils, or crayons.

42 INDIAN MANDALAS COLORING BOOK
by Monika Helwig

Traditionally made of colored rice powder, flowers, leaves, or colored sand, mandalas such as the ones in this book have been used to decorate homes, temples, and meeting places. They may be used daily as well as on special occasions, and are found in the homes of people of all faiths. Each pattern is different and special, increasing the delight of all who see them.

42 MANDALA PATTERNS COLORING BOOK
by Wolfgang Hund

The mandalas in this book mix traditional designs with modern themes. Nature elements such as trees and stars reflect the environment, while animals such as fish, doves, and butterflies remind us we are all part of a universal life. Motifs repeat within mandalas in a soothing way that encourages us to revisit the images, finding new shapes and meanings in them each time. A perfect introduction to the joy of coloring mandalas.

42 SEASONAL MANDALAS COLORING BOOK
by Wolfgang Hund

The seasonal and holiday mandalas in this book will appeal to both the sophisticated and the primal in all of us. Luscious fruit, delicate flowers, leaves and snowflakes are among the nature designs. Holiday themes include bunnies and jack-o-lanterns, Christmas scenes, and New Year's noisemakers. Children can learn about the seasons and celebrate familiar holidays with these playful designs!

>> All mandala books 96 pages ... 42 illus. ... Paperback $11.95

---

101 FAMILY VACATION GAMES: Having Fun while Traveling, Camping or Celebrating at Home *by Shando Varda*

This wonderful collection of games from around the world helps parents to connect with their children. Full of games to play at the beach, on camping trips, in the car, and in loads of other places, including Word Tennis, Treasure Hunt, and Storytelling Starters.

>> 144 pages ... 7 b/w photos ... 43 illus. ... Paperback $14.95 ... Spiral bound $19.95

Free shipping on all personal website orders

More Helpful Books from Hunter House

HELPING HYPERACTIVE KIDS — A SENSORY INTEGRATION APPROACH: Techniques and Tips for Parents and Professionals
by Lynn J. Horowitz, MHS, OT, and Cecile Röst, PT

This is an accessible, practical guide to sensory integration, a drug-free therapy for hyperactive children pioneered at the University of Southern California and the Brain Research Center at UCLA. A treatment based on play, sensory integration helps children absorb and process information, and respond to it appropriately. This nonmedical approach can be used in conjunction with, or as a substitute for, traditional drug treatments. When children begin to function better through sensory integration exercises, it raises their self-esteem, which helps in all areas of their life.

>> 160 pages ... 15 photos ... 19 illus. ... Paperback $14.95

SAFE DIETING FOR TEENS (2nd Edition) *by Linda Ojeda, PhD*

This common-sense approach to weight loss shows teens how to eat sensibly and build muscle and outlines the dangers of yo-yo dieting, anorexia, and bulimia. The emphasis of the book is to help teens lose weight slowly, safely, and as easily as possible. It encourages them to take control of their own health by informing them about what's in the foods they eat and providing many alternatives to higher-fat foods. Based on the author's years of experience and research, it offers tips about what really works and what doesn't. The book addresses the emotional aspect of weight and overeating and asks teens to consider times and triggers that spark splurges and cravings. With calorie and fat counts, a wide range of food plans, and a parents' guide to helping teens diet safely, Linda Ojeda gives teens straightforward advice on making informed health choices about their bodies and themselves.

>> 168 pages ... 1 illus. ... Paperback $14.95

THE WORRIED CHILD: Recognizing Anxiety in Children and Helping Them Heal *by Paul Foxman, PhD*

Anxiety in children affects their physical health and intellectual, emotional, and social development. Today's triggers include an increase in divorce rates, family breakdown, and a failing school system. The result? A shell-shocked generation of children, many of whom suffer from significant anxiety. Dr. Foxman shows that this anxiety is preventable - or can at least be minimized. He explains the importance of adequate rest, sleep, and exercise, and uses lists, exercises, sample dialogues, and case studies to outline steps that can be taken by parents, schools, health professionals, and children themselves.

>> 304 pages ... 2 illus. ... 5 tables ... Paperback $17.95

To order visit www.hunterhouse.com or call (800)-266-5592